S0-BID-645

MILITARY BAND ARRANGING

A Practical Modern Course
for Schools and Private Study

by

WILLIAM C. WHITE

Principal of Music
U. S. Army Music School
Washington, D. C.

CARL FISCHER, INC.
COOPER SQUARE
BOSTON NEW YORK CHICAGO

22998-73

22998-73

CONTENTS

INTRODUCTION

In Part I of this work the good and bad qualities of each instrument used in the Military Band, with information designed to assist the student in scoring intelligently for them, have been pointed out.

The contents of Part II are not based simply on theoretical knowledge but have been tested by actual experience.

There are several excellent books on Orchestration and a few on Military Band Arranging; some of the latter, however, either contain superfluous material or far too little to be of practical use to the student, for the reason that their contents are not classified and, as a consequence, do not present the matter clearly enough to be readily understandable to the beginner.

The necessity for a comprehensive text book on this important subject has therefore become apparent and, as a matter of economy, desirable. The author's apology for presuming to meet this necessity is, that for several years he has been teaching military band arranging in a systematic way, dividing it into five general classifications as set forth in Part II of this book.

Originality is not claimed, but it is believed that the manner in which this important subject is compiled and presented will materially assist the student in overcoming the many difficulties usually met by the novice.

The subject of TRANSPOSITION has not been dealt with for the reason that this, as well as a thorough knowledge of rudiments of music and harmony, must have been acquired before the student can hope to arrange skillfully for the military band.

The following books, to which indebtedness is acknowledged, have been consulted in the preparation of this work:

"The Wind Band and Its Instruments". . . . . *Clappé*
"The Principles of Wind Band Transcription". . . . . *Clappé*
"Orchestration" . . . . *Forsyth*
"Modern Treatise of Orchestration and Instrumentation". . . . *Berlioz*
"Modern Orchestration and Instrumentation" . . . . *Kling*
"The Military Band". . . . . *Miller*
"The Military Band". . . . . *Griffiths*
"The Brass Band". . . . . *Dr. Vincent*
"The Orchestra" . . . . *Prout*

I also desire to extend my thanks to the instructors associated with me at the U. S. Army Music School at Washington, D. C., for their helpful criticisms and cordial coöperation in the preparation of this work.

William C. White,
Washington, D.C.,
January, 1923.

PART ONE

MILITARY BAND INSTRUMENTS

The D♭ Piccolo

The D♭ Piccolo is almost indispensable in the military band, by reason of its being so well adapted to martial music, ballets, and other compositions containing accented rhythms of a decided nature. It has a tonal compass of two octaves and a minor sixth, playing:

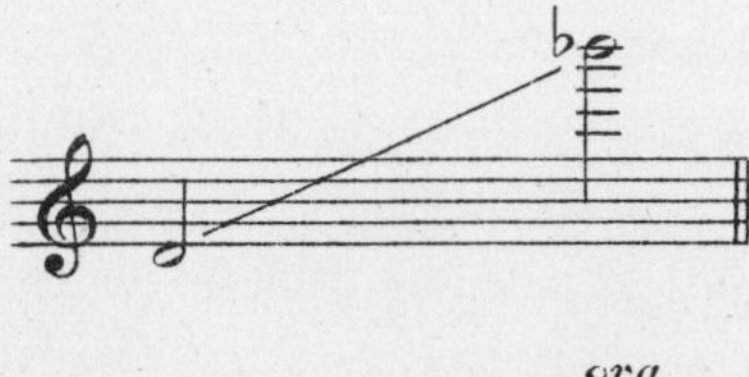

and sounding:

(The tones of the D♭ piccolo sound a minor ninth higher than they are written, and those of the C piccolo an octave higher). The C piccolo is rarely used in military bands.

The most brilliant tones of the piccolo are found between:

Tones lying below this register are weak and colorless and of little value to the military band. From thrice lined F(f^3) and upwards to thrice lined B♭(b^3)*) the tones are shrill and piercing, but nevertheless effective in fortissimo passages.

The piccolo is used very prominently in military marches and popular music and adds a brilliant color, which is very pronounced, to the woodwinds of the band. However, in concert music (except where special effects are desired) the best writers and arrangers score sparingly for it. Professor Kling, in his "Modern Orchestration and Instrumentation" says of

*) *For explanation of pitch names see* "Register of Musical Tones" *p. 36.*

this instrument, "The Piccolo should not be used too frequently; the high notes in particular prove very tiresome to the listener in a short time, owing to the sharp and whistling timbre; its part should, therefore, be well supplied with rests." Kling's suggestion applies to the orchestra only. Still, discretion should always be used when scoring for it in military band arrangements.

The piccolo is a melody instrument, but is almost expressionless, for the reason that its tones lie so high on the band keyboard. It is, therefore, better adapted for the brilliancy of the Scherzo than the slower measure of the Andante. In accompaniments of an arpeggio nature it is a very useful instrument. Many examples of this style may be found in the works of Wagner, Mendelssohn, Liszt, Tschaikowsky and others.

The Boehm system piccolo is really the only practical instrument in this day and age. Nearly all styles of playing which include difficult passages, skips, trills, etc., can be executed upon it with comparative ease.

The piccolo is not an easy instrument to play in tune. It requires considerable humoring and should be placed in the hands of a careful and experienced player, otherwise it will become offensive to sensitive ears, and harrowing to the soul of the bandmaster.

Whenever the piccolo and flute are used together (on the same part) better results, with respect to intonation, could be obtained if both instruments were built in the same key; for example: The C piccolo to be used with the C flute and the D♭ piccolo with the D♭ flute.

FLUTES

Two flutes, pitched respectively in C and D♭, are employed in the military bands of the United States Army. The two instruments are, as a rule, used by one player. Both flutes have a compass of three octaves and a minor second.

The C flute plays:

and sounds as written, while the D♭ flute playing the same notes, sounds a minor 2nd higher, viz:

The best tones of the flute are found between:

The tones below this register are nearly inaudible when played in the military band. From thrice lined D and upwards the tone is very bright and penetrating, and is especially well adapted to vigorous passages. As the fingering upon the Boehm flute (which is the only system recommended) is identical with that of the Boehm piccolo, what has been said of the latter with respect to difficult passages, skips, trills, etc., applies also to the flute. However, it may be well to state that sharp keys present less difficulties to the player of flute and piccolo than do the flat keys. The part for D♭ flute, being notated a semitone lower than for the C flute, affords the performer on that instrument the advantage of playing almost entirely in sharp keys. For example, the following excerpt from the "Third Suite" by Tschaikowsky, (Chappell Edition,) written for the C flute:

--is much easier to play on the D♭ flute, thus:

Other examples of similar character may be found in the "Second Hungarian Rhapsody" by Liszt and "Die Walkure" by Wagner.

As a rule, the flute cannot be considered a solo instrument in the military band for the good and sufficient reason that no combination of wind instruments can be played softly enough for its accompaniment. In combination with reed instruments it finds its true sphere and adds a voice of great value to the military band.

The flute is most generally used in doubling the melody in the higher octave in combination with reed instruments; clarinet, oboe, etc. It is also well adapted to florid passages.

THE B♭ CLARINET

The B♭ Clarinet is the principal instrument of the military band, bearing the same relation thereto that the violin does to the orchestra.

The B♭ Clarinet has an extensive compass of three octaves and a minor sixth.

Playing:

and sounding a full tone lower than written. It has also great flexibility and variety of tone, and lends itself very readily to brilliancy of execution. The compass of the B♭ clarinet is divided into four registers, viz:

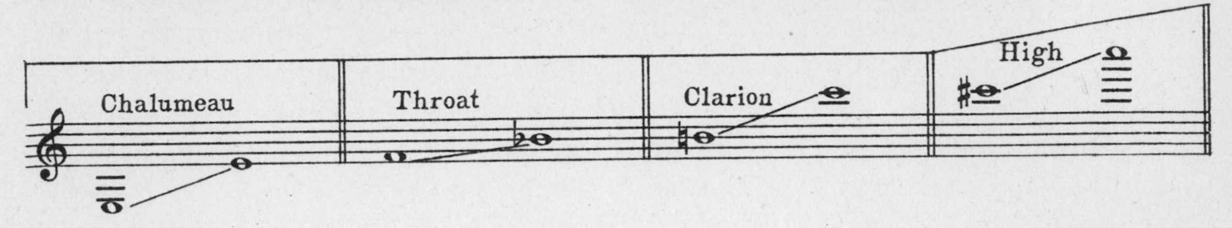

The low sounds of the chalumeau register may be used, with excellent effect, for broad sustained melodies, with all the B♭ clarinets of the band playing in unison; also for accompaniments of an arpeggio nature. The throat register is poor and weak in tone, and, unless care be exercised by the player, those tones will almost invariably be found too sharp in pitch. For this reason it is advisable to avoid as much as possible this register when writing slow and sustained passages for clarinets. The chalumeau register of the E♭ clarinet will cover this weak part of the B♭ very nicely. A point to be remembered by arrangers when scoring.

The clarion register of the B♭ clarinet is the most beautiful part of the instrument. The tones are clear, crisp and brilliant. This register is also well suited to movements of a sympathetic nature.

The high register is very brilliant and penetrating. The upper part of this register must be used with caution; otherwise there will be great deviation from correct pitch. In writing for the high register it is well to make thrice lined F the limit. Still, in fortissimo passages (such as are found in military marches, etc.) thrice lined G, A♭, and A may be employed.

Referring once more to the throat register, the best authorities on clarinet playing are agreed that this register, small as it is, embraces about two-thirds of the difficulty of the instrument. Much of the art of good clarinet playing lies in successfully connecting the chalumeau with the clarion register. The throat register of this instrument, with all its defects, is truly a stumbling block which can only be overcome by long and diligent practice.

A concert band consisting of from forty to forty-five players should have from ten to twelve B♭ clarinets, divided into solo, first, second and third. Two B♭ clarinets to each B♭ cornet or trumpet is apparently the right proportion for military band work.

THE E♭ CLARINET

The E♭ Clarinet is a perfect fourth higher in pitch than the B♭; its range being the same as the latter instrument. It sounds a minor 3rd higher than written. The E♭ clarinet is not a good solo instrument, as it is thinner and weaker in tone than the B♭. It is, nevertheless, a very useful instrument in the military band, being of great assistance to the piccolo in staccato passages and the like; strengthening the flute in sustained melody, and in high passages of valuable aid to the B♭ clarinet; in fact one of the chief functions of the E♭ clarinet is to assist the B♭ clarinets in extreme passages.

Many interesting instances of the E♭ clarinet's effectiveness may be found in the works of Wagner, Mendelssohn, Von Weber, Saint-Saens, etc.

Two E♭ clarinets are ample for a large band (from forty-five players up).

THE E♭ ALTO CLARINET

The E♭ Alto Clarinet is pitched an octave lower than the small E♭ clarinet and a perfect fifth below the B♭.

It plays:

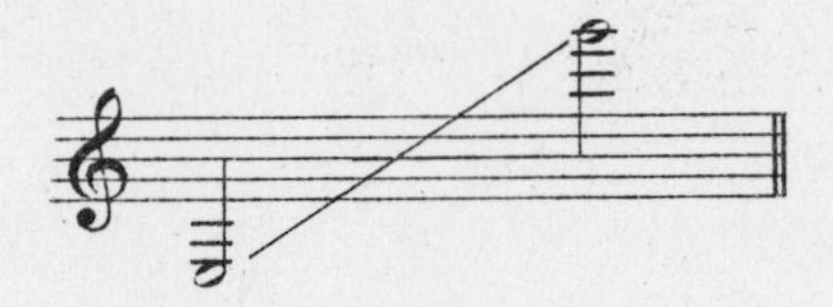

and sounds:

It is a beautiful instrument and, while not so well suited to solo work as the more flexible B♭ clarinet, is a valuable addition to the military band. Its compass is divided into four registers, as on the E♭ and B♭ clarinets, viz: Chalumeau, Throat, Clarion and High, and what has been written respecting the good and bad points of these registers applies also to the Alto clarinet. However, the extreme high tones on the Alto clarinet, viz:

should be employed sparingly, if at all, for the reason that they are hazardous and uncertain, and are difficult to play in tune. The B♭ clarinet can produce these tones without difficulty and with much more purity.

The low tones (chalumeau register) of the Alto clarinet are the richest on the instrument and most marked in character.

A pair of Alto clarinets is necessary in large bands containing forty or more players. In band arrangements transcribed from orchestra scores, the Viola parts may be allotted to the Alto clarinets and french horns with fine effect.

22998-73

The Alto clarinet blends well with the french horn and is of valuable assistance to it in high or quick solos. It also softens the melody when combined with the baritone or euphonium, and, in band arrangements that do not contain Alto clarinet parts, can be used very effectively to reinforce the first bassoon parts which, in large bands, are likely to be overbalanced. The Alto clarinet is written for in the treble clef and is therefore a transposing instrument.

THE B♭ BASS CLARINET

The B♭ Bass Clarinet, pitched an octave below the ordinary B♭ Clarinet, plays:

and sounds:

Its value to the military band is great, in fact, indispensable. It forms the natural bass to the clarinet choir and is of equal importance to the military band as are the cellos to the concert orchestra. The cello part is, whenever practicable, nearly always assigned to it when making band arrangements from orchestra scores. It is of valuable assistance to the second bassoon in band arrangements that do not contain bass clarinet parts. One bass clarinet and one alto clarinet supplementing the bassoons, not only strengthen the parts for these instruments without covering up the distinctive tone color of the double reed, but are of great assistance in keeping the bassoons in tune.

Bass clarinet parts are written in the treble clef, (except in German arrangements). It thus becomes a transposing instrument. The advantage of writing bass clarinet parts in the treble clef lies in the fact that bandsmen playing that instrument can, without difficulty in the reading and fingering, play any other member of the clarinet family. Extreme low tones, on both alto and bass clarinet, sound much better when emitted slowly. Quick slurred or detached passages like the following (nominal pitch) are not considered practicable:

Until quite recently, the majority of American band arrangers and band masters have classed alto and bass clarinets as unessential instruments, not having in mind, perhaps, the absolute necessity of employing the entire family or choir of clarinets in the military band. The string elements of the orchestra would indeed be incomplete and altogether deficient without its violas and cellos. It is quite as essential that the clarinet choir be complete in the band, viz: E♭, B♭, E♭ alto and B♭ bass, as it is considered desirable that the quartet of strings shall form the basis of an orchestra. The advantage of employing, in the military band, all members of the complete clarinet choir consists in being able to use homogeneously one register color throughout an extended chord. The chalumeau register has a very marked character of dark, reedy, and somewhat sinister coloring. If the following chord were scored as follows:

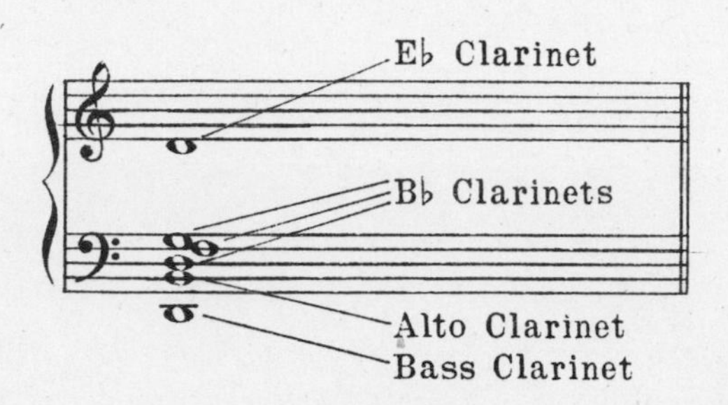

each note of the harmony would be sounded in the richest part of the chalumeau register of the clarinet choir. If, however, we lacked an E♭ clarinet and the upper note of the chord were played by a B♭ clarinet it would lie above the most characteristic part of the chalumeau register of that instrument. The same situation would obtain if we lacked an alto clarinet and the note great B were taken by a bass clarinet.

Professor H. Kling in his work on "Modern Orchestration and Instrumentation" has the following to say about the incomparable alto and bass clarinets: "The beauty, uniformity, and great pliancy of tonal character possessed by both the alto clarinet in E♭ and the bass clarinet in B♭, subdues the tonal volume of the higher wood and especially the brass instruments, to such an extent as to impart an even and euphonious tonal quality to the entire instrumental masses of the military band, and I cannot understand why they are not included in every band; it is certainly to be regretted that they are not brought into more general use, as a very important part of the different tonal types, necessary for the artistic blending of the wind instruments, is lost thereby. Apart from the advantage, brought about by the perfected mechanism of these instruments, of producing transcriptions and arrangements of symphonic works of both classic and modern masters for military band, in their complete harmonic and instrumental entirety; in such a manner as to render the technical difficulties contained therein possible for both the conductor and his men after conscientious and repeated study, a wealth of tonal shadings could be produced, which is entirely unknown at the present time, and which would approach considerably near to the character and tonal quality of orchestra music."

THE OBOE

The Oboe is of great value to the military band. It is very effective as a solo instrument and combines well with flutes, clarinets, horns, bassoons, flugel horns and saxophones. In combination with the french horn (the oboe playing the upper octave) it is particularly pleasing.

The oboe has a compass of about two octaves and a diminished 5th, playing:

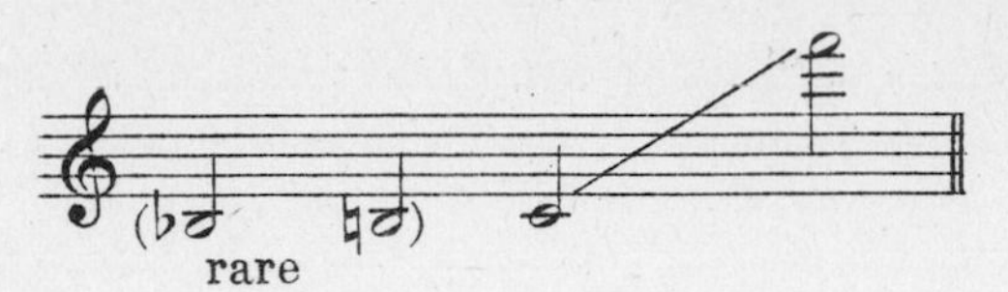

and sounding as written.

Its best tones are found between:

From the thrice lined C and upward the tones are sharp and cutting and not of any value to the general ensemble. In its lowermost register, from once lined A downward, the tones are somewhat coarse and rough, but are nevertheless use ful to the military band.

Oboes may well be employed in pairs. In fact, a concert band consisting of forty or more players should have two oboes. Oboes used in connection with flutes in sustained harmonies are very effective. They impart a quality of tone to the general ensemble that stands out so well from the instruments they are supporting that to be without them would deprive the reed section of a voice of unusual beauty and variety. For example, see extract from Beethoven's "Leonore Overture No. 3."

Another example similar to the above may be found in Mendelssohn's Overture "Calm Sea and Happy Voyage."

While the oboe is very effective as a solo instrument, it should, for open air playing, be supported by a flute or clarinet. The penetrating quality of the oboe will stand out well from either of these instruments, so there need be no hesitation in selecting one or the other to support it.

It is quite possible for a first rate player to execute detached staccato passages on the oboe. However, it should not be used too frequently on that style of articulation for the reason that legato playing is more expressive of the true character of the instrument.

Oboes very effectively depict music of a simple pastoral nature and are also well adapted to joyous and humorous scenes. Many of the old as well as modern composers have used this instrument extensively in their works.

THE BASSOON

The Bassoon forms the natural bass to the oboe.

Like the oboe, it is played with a double reed, but being a larger instrument with a broader reed, it is easier to blow. The bassoon has a practical compass of three octaves.

Playing:

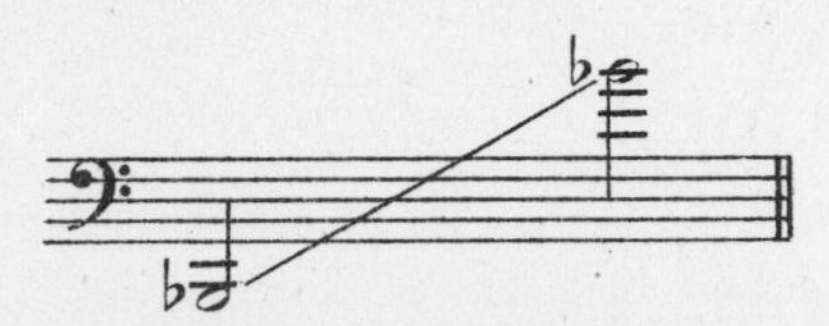

and sounding as written.

Its best tones are found between:

While the tones lying immediately above those illustrated are devoid of any particular character, from once lined D to once lined A the quality is very fine and quite similar to the human voice. (Bassoon parts are written in both the bass and tenor clefs).

Skips and arpeggios can be executed upon the bassoon in all keys; rapid passages are easy in the middle register. In moderate tempo, staccato passages are very effective. Legato playing, however, is the true articulation for the bassoon. Keys containing many sharps or flats are more or less difficult.

Two bassoons should be employed, as first and second, in military bands; the second sometimes assisting the brass basses. Both bassoons are also very effective when used on the inner parts of the harmony and blend well with the baritone and euphonium in sustained melodies.

Bassoon parts may be supplemented by alto and bass clarinets. The result thus obtained produces a fine melodic effect analogous to that of orchestra 'cellos playing in unison.

For outdoor playing the doubling of each bassoon part with an alto and bass clarinet is very effective and really essential, for the reason that bassoons are not in themselves sufficient bass for the wood-winds of a military band. Even in the modern orchestra the bass of the wood-wind family consists of bassoons, contra-bassoons and a bass clarinet. This proves without doubt that if two bassoons are insufficient bass for the wood-winds of the orchestra, how inadequate they must be to uphold that office in the military band, which possesses a much larger wood-wind section than the modern orchestra.

Tschaikowsky, in his "Pathetic Symphony," employed the great range of the bassoon with fine effect, and has thereby shown, as have other modern writers, that this magnificent instrument is a heavy tragedian, thus contradicting the statement made by so many writers that "the bassoon is fit only to depict music of a comic or humorous nature."

SARRUSOPHONES

The Sarrusophone family consists of B♭ Soprano, E♭ Alto, B♭ Tenor, E♭ Baritone, B♭ Bass and E♭ Contra Bass, and has a collective compass of over five octaves, viz:

(Sarrusophones are played with a double reed).

Their tone is nasal and coarse. The inventor, Sarrus, a French bandmaster, appears to have had the idea in mind to provide the military band with instruments of double-reed tonal characteristics, wherein the sonority should be greater than that of oboe or bassoon. In point of sonority he succeeded, but failed in his effort to obtain a tone of equal purity with the more delicate oboes and bassoons.

The most useful of all the sarrusophones for military band work is the E♭ Contra Bass, which, on account of its great flexibility and powerful low tones, is very effective when supplementing the brass basses in large military bands. Its compass is:

It softens and rounds out the harsher tones of the brass basses and blends splendidly with them. Sarrusophones are essentially legato in their characteristics and are quite at home in scale and arpeggio passages.

SAXOPHONES

The Saxophone is a modern hybrid instrument, invented by Adolphe Sax, having a mouthpiece similar to that of the clarinet (single reed), applied to a conical brass tube. In general appearance the saxophone resembles the bass clarinet. However, the tube of the latter instrument is made of wood and is cylindrical in shape. Owing to its conical bore, the series of harmonics on the saxophone differ from those of the clarinet. The saxophone, when overblown, gives rise to the even numbers of the harmonic series and produces an octave above the fundamental. The saxophone, similar to the oboe, etc., is therefore one of the class known as octave instruments. On the other hand, the clarinet, being a cylindrical tube closed at one end by a reed, acts on the principle of a stopped organ pipe, which, when overblown, gives rise to the uneven numbers of the harmonic series and produces a 12th above its fundamental.

The saxophone family, or choir, consists of B♭ Soprano, E♭ Alto, B♭ Tenor, E♭ Baritone and B♭ Bass. They have a collective compass of four octaves and a perfect fourth, sounding:

at actual (concert) pitch.

Saxophones are notated in the treble clef and therefore become transposing instruments. The B♭ Soprano sounding one full tone lower, the E♭ Alto a minor sixth, the B♭ Tenor one octave and a major second, the E♭ Baritone one octave and a minor sixth and the B♭ Bass two octaves and a major second lower than written. The individual range of the entire family of saxophones is given herewith:

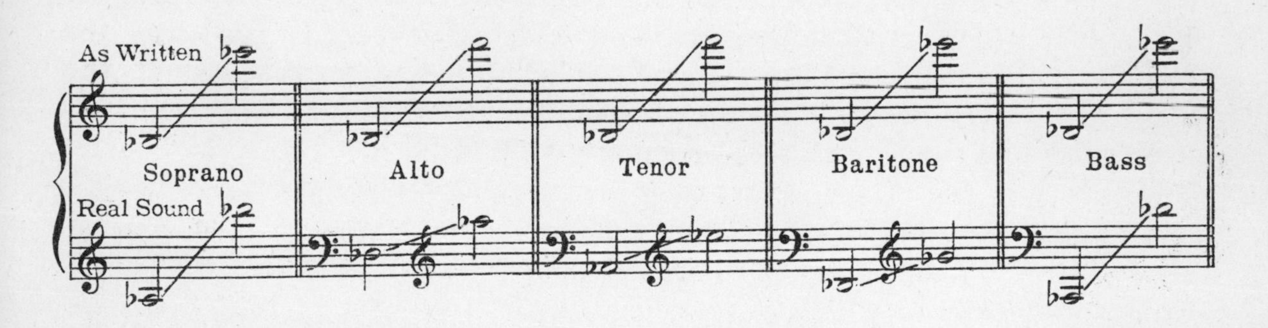

The chief difficulty in saxophone playing lies in the ability to produce a fine tone and to play in tune. The finger technic is comparatively easy, being almost identical with that of the Boehm system flute.

In the lower major third of the saxophone register (from small B♭ to once lined D, nominal pitch), the tone is loud and coarse and difficult to produce, especially pianissimo. When scoring for saxophones, those tones should be avoided as much as possible, the only exception being fortissimo passages.

Trills are easy and very effective throughout the entire compass of the saxophone, excepting whole tone trills on the following:

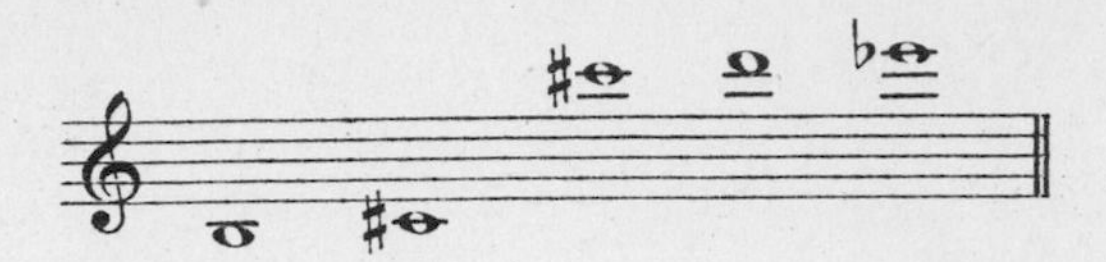

The best saxophones for military band use are the E♭ Alto, the B♭ Tenor and the E♭ Baritone. Their tonal quality may be described as follows: The E♭ Alto is soft, brilliant, and well suited for solo playing. The B♭ Tenor is expressive and melancholy and quite adapted to passages of a sentimental and cantabile nature. The E♭ Baritone, somewhat hollow and harsh in the lowermost part of its register, may be used to good advantage in supplementing the euphonium or E♭ bass. The B♭ Soprano and the B♭ Bass saxophones would make valuable additions to large bands (from forty players up).The B♭ Soprano, while somewhat shrill in its high register, is an excellent instrument in the hands of a good player and becomes very useful in marching music. The B♭ Bass saxophone should be used to supplement the brass basses. It rounds out, to a great extent, the bass section of a large band. However, its tone is too heavy for fine work. The contra-bass sarrusophone, already noted, is a much better reed bass than the bass saxophone, being more agile and much softer and smoother in tone than the latter instrument.

Saxophones, when used as a quartet or choir in the military band, possess great power and volume and in the hands of first rate performers are smooth and effective. As a connecting link between the wood-winds and the brass of the military band they are very valuable, serving to increase the volume of the reed and flute element and subduing to a great extent the harshness of the brass. They make beautiful and smooth that which before was harsh and rough, and blend perfectly with brass and reed alike. Charles Vincent, Mus., Doc., Oxon, England, in his work on the "Brass Band," has the following to say about them: "Though these characteristic instruments are made of brass and are suited to brass bands, they are really reed instruments. Their addition to large bands is most strongly urged on account of their beautiful yet weird quality of tone. The combination of a quartet or of the entire family of saxophones is simply marvelous. They bring to a band a tone quality which when once introduced can never be dispensed with."

Similarly with all single reed instruments, saxophones are better adapted to legato rather than to staccato articulation. In scale and arpeggio passages their possibilities nearly equal those of the clarinet. However, the breadth of tone inherent in the saxophone choir seems to indicate movements of a cantabile nature as the best sphere in which their characteristics may be displayed. There, and in sustained harmonies, saxophones chiefly excel.

In small bands, where alto and bass clarinets and bassoons are not employed, the alto and tenor saxophones make very good substitutes for those instruments. The baritone saxophone is also a fair substitute for the bassoon. In old band arrangements that do not contain alto and bass clarinet or bassoon parts, the saxophones may be distributed as follows: Soprano with the B♭ cornets. Alto with the solo E♭ alto or saxhorn. Tenor with the brass baritone, and the Baritone and Bass saxophones with the brass basses. When saxophones are employed as substitutes for alto and bass clarinets and bassoons they should be allotted to careful players for the reason that they are of a different timbre and much heavier sounding than the more delicate wood reed instruments.

Although saxophones make good substitutes for the various instruments already mentioned, special parts should by all means be written for them, as is the case in modern band scores. Their real value to the military band then becomes readily apparent, whether they are used in combination with small groups of reed and brass or to strengthen the whole ensemble.

NOTE: – The C Melody saxophone – pitched one octave below the oboe – is used extensively in cafe and dance orchestras. Its use in the Military Band, however, has not yet been adopted; perhaps for the reason that its register is well overlapped by the E♭ Alto and B♭ Tenor saxophones. Further, it does not add a new variety of tone color to the Saxophone family previously described.

CORNETS

The Cornet is a military development or transformation of the old post horn. Its tubing is partly cylindrical and partly conical. The bore is larger than that of the trumpet and a cup-shaped mouthpiece is used. In the cornet mouthpiece there are no angles at the bottom of the cup which curve into the bore, as is the case with the trumpet, therefore the tone of the cornet, while being easier to produce, is a looser quality than that of the trumpet.

Modern cornets are built in E flat, B flat, C and A. The B flat is the only one now in use in military bands. The E flat cornet is the proper leading instrument for brass bands, which are now almost a thing of the past in the United States.

THE B♭ CORNET

The B flat cornet has a compass of two octaves and diminished fifth, playing:

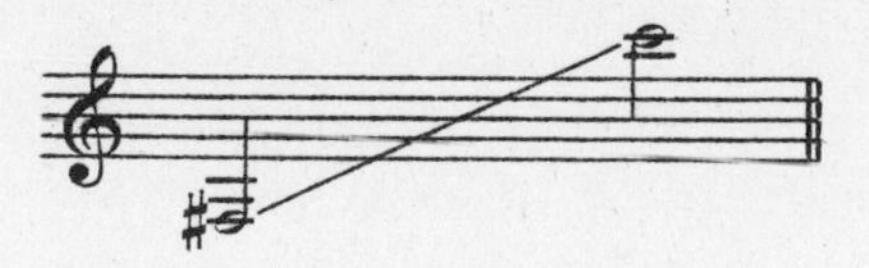

and sounding:

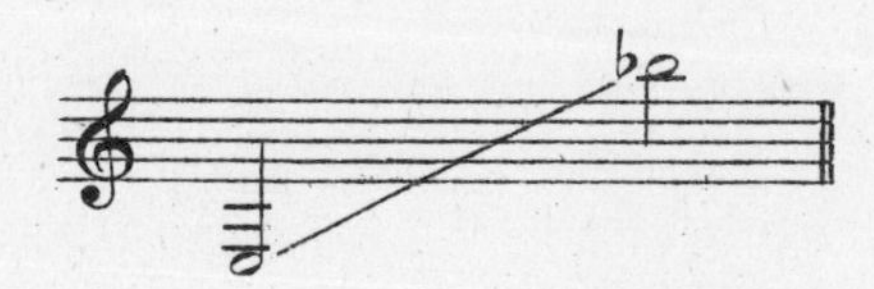

The compass of the cornet may be divided into three registers as follows:

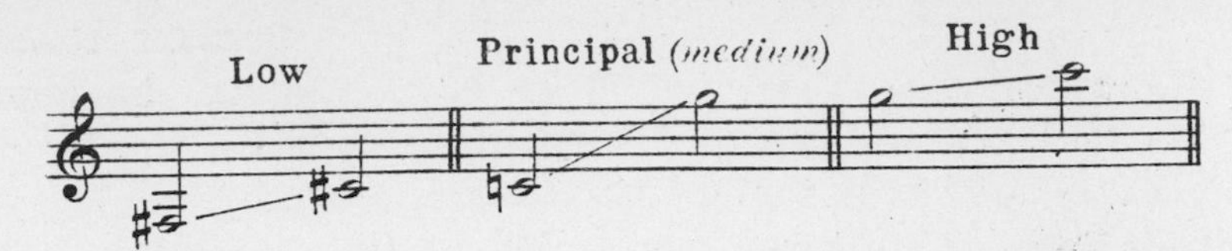

In the low register the tone is coarse and dull, and difficult to play in tune, due to certain discrepancies in the valve, or piston, system, which the modern maker cannot eradicate (See Chapter IV "The Wind Band and its Instruments" Clappé). The best sounding notes are found in the principal or medium register. The high register is more or less strident and practicable only for first rate players and soloists.

The B flat cornet is invaluable as a solo instrument. However, while it blends well with all the brass instruments, great care must be taken by arrangers in using it to support other instruments, in which capacity it is not nearly so well suited as the B flat flugelhorn or trumpet. In song transcriptions and solos that are required to stand out strongly, the cornet is superior to the trumpet. For fanfare and solos of a bravura nature the trumpet is the premier.

The cornet is easier to play than the trumpet; it speaks more freely and is better adapted for high music; it can play passages or melodies without becoming obtrusive, still, it should never replace the trumpet whenever the characteristics of the latter are required.

Scale passages and groups of notes may easily be played legato on the cornet. Intervals and chords (legato) are more difficult but not impossible. The chief forte of the cornet, however, is the staccato style of articulation in single, double and triple tonguing.

Most trills below:

are bad sounding or difficult.

A table of difficult trills lying above that register is given herewith:

To sum up, it may be said that trills are easy of execution upon the cornet provided they do not involve cross fingering; in other words, if they can be produced by the manipulation of one finger they are practicable. In band scoring, however, trills are not, as a rule, written in the cornet parts unless some very special effect is desired, in which case the arranger should be sure that the trill occurs on some good note in the principal (medium) register and can be played with ease.

THE B♭ FLUGELHORN

The Flugelhorn is a descendant of the old key bugle. It is named from the fact that the player of that instrument in German regimental brass bands marched at the right hand corner of the front rank and was known as the flugelmann. This instrument is called the bugle in France and Belgium and occupies the same position in the bands of those countries as the cornet does in the United States. The flugelhorn is a conical bore instrument and has a very wide bell. It is played with a deep cupped mouthpiece and possesses a clear characteristic tone of much beauty. In the brass bands of England this instrument has long been a favorite. Its usefulness to military bands, however, should not be overlooked, for the reason that it supplies a voice of distinctive color to the brass section of the band.

The compass and pitch of the B flat flugelhorn is the same as the B♭ cornet. While the flugelhorn cannot compare with the cornet as a solo instrument, it is infinitely better than that instrument when used in combination with reeds and horns, imparting richness to melodic and legato passages and blending well with the general ensemble. In this capacity it also outrivals the trumpet.

The technical possibilities of the flugelhorn are identical with those of the cornet.

THE B♭ TRUMPET

The B♭Trumpet has a practical compass identical with the B♭ cornet; it also has the same length of tubing as the B♭ cornet and the B♭ flugelhorn, but the form of the tube differs from those instruments in that it is narrower, and cylindrical in two-thirds and conical in one-third of its length. By reason of this smaller diameter of its tube, the harmonics or overtones are more clearly voiced than in the cornet and other brass instruments of similar bore. For this reason the trumpet is more brilliant than the cornet or flugelhorn.

In combination with other instruments, reed and brass, trumpets are preferable to cornets, both in melody and harmony. In combination with trombones, they form the natural trumpet choir, so indispensable to the military band. As already stated, the trumpet is more brilliant than the cornet, owing to its upper partials (harmonics) being more prominent. On the other hand, the cornet is more sonorous than the trumpet and is likely to be overblown by amateurs, thereby producing a coarse, disagreeable effect.

The tone of the trumpet blends well with that of the french horn, the clarinet, and the trombone. When combined with the french horns it produces a chivalrous quality of tone, a very fine example of which may be found in Act II, Scene 3, of "Lohengrin," Wagner.

All the great masters from Bach and Handel to Verdi and Wagner have produced excellent effects in their works through the correct and appropriate application of the trumpet. An exceptional example of such usage is shown in the "Marches Aux Flambeaux" No. 1 and 2 (Military Band Arrangement) by Meyerbeer.

When muted effects are desired in the production of chorals, hymns (church music) and the like, muted trumpets used in combination with muted trombones or muted french horns are very effective, but for fanfares and music of a brilliant or tragic character the use of muted trumpets is not recommended, for the reason that a toy trumpet effect which is anything but noble and brilliant will result.

THE E♭ TRUMPET

The practical compass of the E♭ Trumpet is:

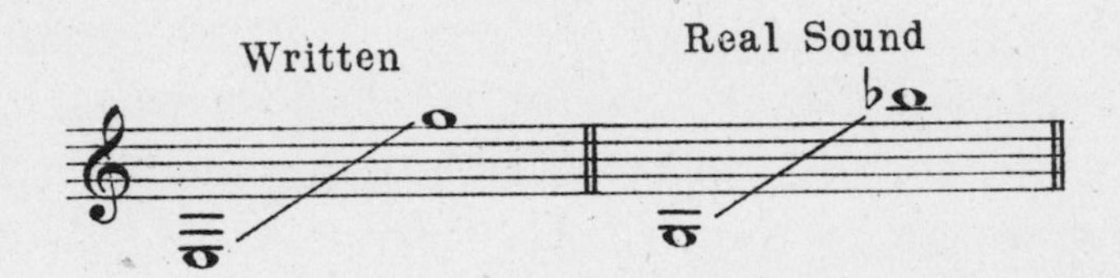

It sounds a minor 3rd higher (at actual pitch) than written. This fact should be kept in mind when scoring for the E♭ trumpet, or re-writing E♭ trumpet parts to be played on the B♭ trumpets, which are the only ones used in the bands of the United States. Although the E♭ trumpet is still scored for in the band journals of various foreign countries which find their way into our libraries, it has never been popular with American bandsmen, perhaps for the reason that the parts assigned to it are uninteresting, and there is no demand for players on that instrument.

There seems to be no reason why the E♭ trumpet, awkward and uninteresting as it is, should not pass into disuse altogether, and in its place the more facile and easily comprehended trumpet in B♭ be scored for, since the B♭ trumpets well overlap the range of the B♭ trombones and are the natural complement of the "Brass" register.

FRENCH HORNS

The modern French Horn, with 3 valves, has a chromatic compass of three octaves, viz:

The tones below:

are possible, but unsteady, difficult of enunciation, and not effective in military band arrangements, and those lying above:

should not be written in military band horn parts, except in solo passages. Modern orchestra writers often exceed these limits however and cover the whole range of the horn, some excellent examples of which may be found in the works of Tschaikowsky, Dvořák, Grainger and Rachmaninoff.

The orchestral horns now in use are pitched in F; also in B♭. Those for military band in E♭ and F. The employment of the B♭ horn in the military band would be a great asset. It is easier to play on high parts than either the E♭ or F horn, and for this reason would fit remarkably well on the 1st horn parts.

A good arrangement would be to have two B♭ horns playing the high parts (1st and 3rd) and two E♭ or F horns the low (2nd and 4th).

A scale of the "open" tones on the E♭, F, and B♭ horns, nominally the same, together with the actual sounds produced, is given herewith. The gaps between the "open" notes are filled up by the use of the valves.

Ranges of the different french horns

From the foregoing it will be readily seen that the name of the horn (E♭, F, or B♭) indicates the fundamental tone given by it.

A quartet of horns is necessary to the military band. The parts are usually written in pairs, i. e., 1st and 2nd on one part and 3rd and 4th on the other. Great care should be taken when scoring for french horns, as properly arranged horn parts, with attention given to the correct distribution of the notes of the chord and judicious doubling of the right notes, do much toward making the inner parts sound well in the band.

It is generally recognized among horn players that the 1st and 3rd should play upon small mouthpieces to make the higher notes easier of production, and the 2nd and 4th upon larger ones in order that the lower notes may come out fuller and better.

Excellent effects may be obtained from the horns, sometimes with one pair, but more often with the whole quartet, by a judicious employment of sustained notes. Indeed, this style of playing is the true sphere of the french horn. Slow solos and sustained passages are very effective when played by the french horn, as are also Hunting Strains. The latter may be played with great rapidity upon the "open notes." Very quick passages that involve the use of valves, however, are apt to be indistinct and should be avoided altogether, unless the horn be supported by some other instrument, such as the alto clarinet.

In melodies, the horn may be employed as a support for other instruments, as it adds a softening effect of much beauty. The effect of four horns in unison is very fine indeed.

When scoring for french horns, trills are seldom employed, as they are of no artistic value to the ensemble.

SAXHORNS

The Saxhorn family comprises seven (7) members, viz: E♭ Sopranino, B♭ Soprano, E♭ Alto, B♭ Baritone, B♭ Bass, E♭ Bass, and BB♭ Bass, and are played with a cupped mouthpiece. They were invented by Adolphe Sax, and are practically an application of the valve mechanism to instruments of the Flugel family (called bugles in France and Belgium).

The E♭ Sopranino and B♭ Soprano are used extensively in France, and take parts which in the United States are assigned to E♭ and B♭ cornet. Soprano saxhorns are superior to cornets in that their tone is more mellow and full. This condition arises from the fact that the mouthpiece of the Soprano saxhorn is deeper from lip to throat than that of the cornet. It also has a larger bore.

The five remaining members of the family, viz: the E♭ alto, B♭ bass, B♭ baritone, E♭ bass, and BB♭ bass, are in general use in nearly all military bands.

THE E♭ ALTO

The E♭ Alto, while being superseded to a great extent by french horns in the modern band, is nevertheless a very useful instrument in mounted (Cavalry) bands. In the ordinary marching band it seems that the E♭ alto is a surer instrument and preferable to the french horn, as the latter is very difficult to control unless the embouchre can be kept steady. For concert work, however, the reverse is true and the E♭ alto should be discarded entirely. The E♭ alto has a compass of two octaves and a diminished fifth, playing:

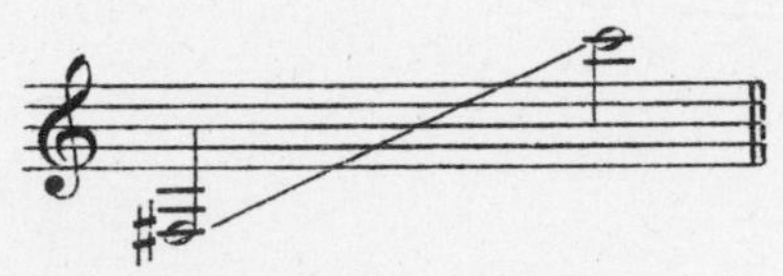

and sounding:

Its chief function is to play accompanying parts, after beats, etc. As a solo instrument, it is of little value. In writing for the E♭ alto it is well to keep within the limits of its "Principal" register. (See Cornets).

The technical possibilities of the E♭ alto are almost identical with those of the B♭ cornet.

When altos are used in lieu of french horns in the band, four are necessary. The parts are written as for french horns, i.e., 1st and 2nd on one part, and 3rd and 4th on the other. The proper distribution of the notes of a chord in band arranging applies equally to altos and french horns (see "French Horns,"). In purely brass arrangements the E♭ alto is useful and, it may be said, necessary, as it supplies the true alto voice to the Saxhorn (Flugel) family and blends splendidly with them all.

THE B♭ BARITONE

The B♭ Baritone, called B♭ Althorn, B♭ Tenor horn, and B♭ Saxhorn, in various European countries, is generally used as a melody instrument, for which purpose it is well adapted. However, it would make a splendid support for the low tones of the french horns and trombones These latter instruments have to deal with inner harmonies and can well bear reinforcement.

The tone quality of the B♭ baritone stands between that of the trombone and the euphonium in the same manner as the tone quality of the cornet stands between the trumpet and flugelhorn. The nominal compass of the B♭ baritone is identical with all saxhorns, viz:

Playing:

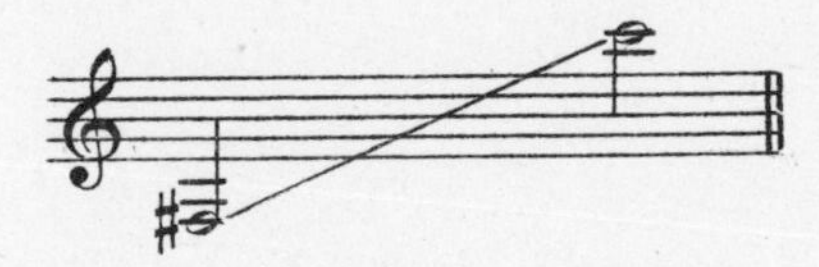

and sounding:

Alto, Tenor, and Baritone solos, Italian style, come out well on this instrument, and passages of extreme rapidity and difficulty can be played up on it, if not too low. As already stated, it is chiefly a melody instrument, but is of great aid to french horns and trombones in inner parts. In unisonal passages with the B♭ clarinet, the baritone playing an octave lower, the effect is very beautiful. It also blends well with the bassoons and bass clarinets.

THE EUPHONIUM

The Euphonium is identical in pitch with the B♭ baritone, but by reason of its larger tubing, its tone is stronger and more voluminous, especially in the lower register. Being equipped with a 4th valve the chromatic compass of the euphonium is extended an augmented 4th lower than the baritone, playing:

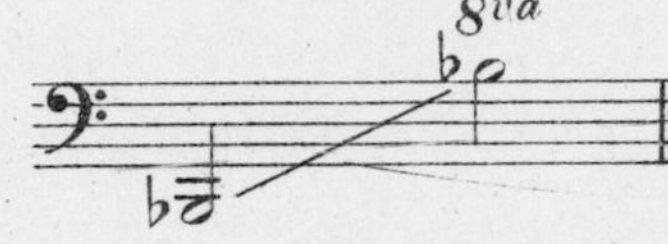

and sounding as written. It is therefore a non-transposing instrument. In military and brass bands the employment of the euphonium is similar to that of the 'cello in the orchestra. As a solo instrument in the band it is equal in importance to the cornet.

As the tone of the euphonium can always be easily distinguished from among the mass of instruments playing in ensemble, attention should be directed toward writing only independent and effective passages, counter or bass melodies, for it. Unisonal bass passages should always be written for the euphonium, and declamatory phrases are entirely suited to its genus. In fact, passages of all kinds, except in the lowermost part of its register, sound well. In small combinations of reed and horn, the euphonium affords an ample and excellent bass. It also makes a good brass substitute for bassoon parts.

The open tones of the euphonium are:

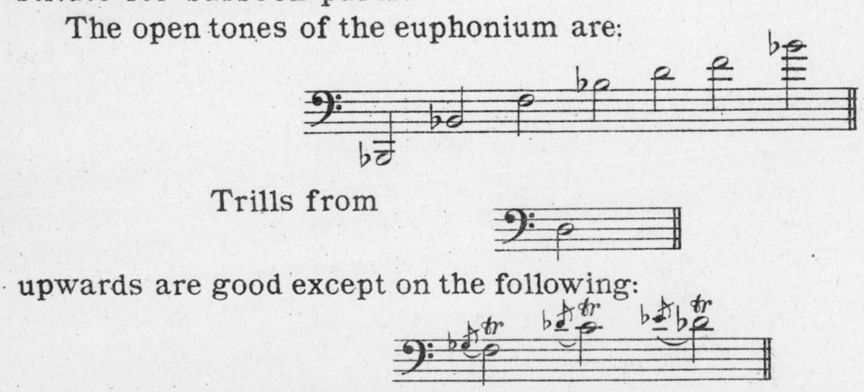

Trills from

upwards are good except on the following:

The legato and staccato style of articulation is easy on the euphonium, but double and triple tonguing is not practicable, and should be avoided when scoring for it.

TROMBONES

Trombones are built in E♭ Alto, B♭ Tenor, F or G Bass, and B♭ Contra Bass. The B♭ and F are the only ones used in American bands (to be more correct, the F trombone now in use is really a B♭ trombone with an F attachment).

The B♭ Tenor Trombone has a chromatic compass of two octaves and a diminished fifth, viz:

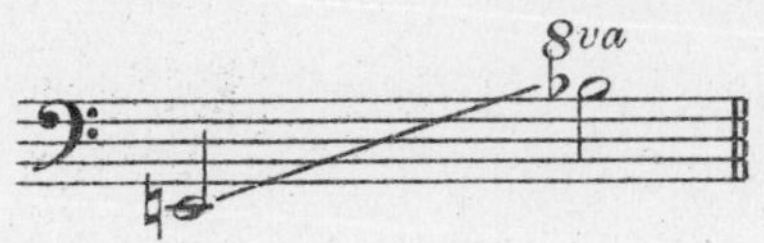

sounding as written.

The F attachment extends the entire compass downward a perfect fourth. Also, some difficult passages on the B♭ trombone are facilitated by the use of the F attachment.

There are seven positions on the slide trombone, each giving a theoretical fundamental tone and its upper partials a semitone lower than the last, and corresponding to the seven positions or shifts on all brass instruments with three valves. These seven positions are found by lengthening the slide a little more for each one, the first position being that in which the slide remains closed. The table of harmonics for the seven positions of the B♭ Tenor Trombone is herewith given:

TABLE OF HARMONICS OF B♭ TROMBONE

They furnish a complete chromatic compass of two octaves and a diminished 5th. The table represents all the tones in practical use. The pedal tones are not practicable, and are used only by soloists where special effects are desired.

The seventh harmonic, marked (x)being too flat and not in tune with our tempered scale, is not used in practice in the closed position. On the other positions, viz., second, third, fourth, fifth, sixth and seventh, the discrepancy may be corrected by use of the slide.Those tones, however, will be found in other positions on the trombone.

The B♭ trombone has a full rich quality suitable for heroic, majestic music, but the tone depends greatly upon the performer's method of playing. The modern tendency to produce a harsh, noisy blare should be condemned.

Besides the B♭ slide trombone, which is most largely used, there are the B♭ valve trombones. They are made in the same key as the B♭ slide, and are constructed in a similar manner, except that the slide is replaced by three pistons, thus enabling the performer to obtain greater technical execution. However, the tone of the valve trombone has not the characteristic timbre of the slide, and is therefore not popular with American bandmasters and bandsmen.

A chart showing the positions of the B♭ slide trombone and the parallel on valve or piston instruments follows:

CHART OF COMPARATIVE POSITIONS OF TROMBONE AND VALVE INSTRUMENTS

B♭ TROMBONE	BARITONE, VALVE TROMBONE AND EUPHONIUM
1st Position (closed)	Open (O)
2nd Position	2nd Valve (2)
3rd Position	1st Valve (1)
4th Position	1st and 2nd Valves (12 or 3rd)
5th Position	2nd and 3rd Valves (23)
6th Position	1st and 3rd Valves (13)
7th Position	1st, 2nd and 3rd Valves (123)

When the F attachment is used, the 7th position is practically lost, as the slide positions become greater than on the B♭. Therefore, parts for the F trombone should not be written below:

Three trombone parts are written in military band arrangements, viz: first, second, and third (or Bass) trombone, and are quite sufficient for a concert band of from 25 to 35 players. The parts allotted to these incomparable instruments are, as a rule, accompanying figures, expressive, grand and religious melodies, unisonal bass passages, etc. For triumphal marches, in fact for every composition of a martial character, trombones are tremendously effective.

When four trombones are used for concert work, it is advisable to double on the third part and thereby strengthen the basses of the band. In large marching bands, six trombones may be used very effectively, two instruments playing on each part.

Rapid passages in any key are difficult, although some of our modern trombone players can perform with astonishing agility. Such passages should not extend beyond the lowest open tone (great B♭) nor higher than once lined D, viz:

For inner (harmony) parts, chords, etc., it is well not to write below small F or E flat or above once lined B flat or F, but for unisonal passages performed by euphoniums, basses, trombones, etc., the whole register of the trombone may be employed with fine effect. The slide trombone, like all other members of the trumpet family, possesses noble and heroic qualities. Forte may be played on the trombone without vulgarity and pianissimo may be produced with great distinctness.

On sustained tones (*p* and *pp*) trombones can be employed to excellent advantage.

Legato playing and slow movements are best suited to the trombones. Double and triple tonguing, lip trills, etc., are possible but are only attempted by artists. They are not practicable or effective in band work.

The tones of the trombone are not fixed and require a good ear for accurate intonation. The performer being just as dependent on a keen ear for finding correct positions as a violinist.

The musical use of trombones has been extensive since Bach and Handel. Mozart fully appreciated them. Beethoven employed them to perfection. The effect of the trombone chords (*pp*) in his Benedictus in the Mass in D is very beautiful. In the Trio and Finale of his ninth symphony the trombones are extensively and effectively used. Other excellent examples may be found in Schubert's Symphonies (especially the one in C), Mendelssohn's "Hymn of Praise," Schumann's "First Symphony" and Wagner's "Flying Dutchman."

BASSES

Basses, or bombardons, (English) are built in F, E flat, C, and Contra B flat. They are pitched lower than other brass valve instruments, an example of which follows: The F bass one octave lower than the F horn, the E flat bass one octave lower than the E flat alto or horn, the C bass a minor third lower than the E flat bass, and the contra B flat bass or (BB flat bass so called) one octave lower than the B flat euphonium.

Basses may be considered as a group by themselves, apart from the saxhorn group, which are more particularly a series of instruments of the bugle or flugel type, ranging from soprano and baritone in compass. The reason for this isolated classification, with respect to basses, is, that valves were applied to this type before the date of Sax's improvements. The upright models of basses, however, may be classed as saxhorns in so far as their shape or model is concerned. The bass and contra-bass valve instruments are the natural development of the now obsolete bass horns and ophicleides; the distinctive feature by which they stand differentiated from the bugle type being the free use of the pedal octave lying between the first and second harmonics. The name bass tuba (bombardon) is usually given to an instrument having for its pedal note the F or E flat of the 16-foot octave, and the name contra bass to an instrument in CC or BB flat a fifth lower. A table of the open notes of the four basses named is given herewith:

The 7th harmonic marked (×) is always flat, as on all brass instruments, and should not be used as an open tone in practice.

American bands employ only two brass basses, the E flat and the BB flat. They are scored for in the bass clef and therefore become non-transposing instruments. The parts written for them sounding at actual pitch. The E flat bass with three valves has a chromatic compass of two octaves and a diminished fifth, viz:

The addition of a fourth valve extends the chromatic compass downward, as follows:

However, these deeper sounds made possible by the fourth valve, require a well-developed embouchure, and are too difficult for the ordinary player. Contra B flat is about the lowest sound that can be easily and clearly produced on the E flat bass. Rapid passages below:

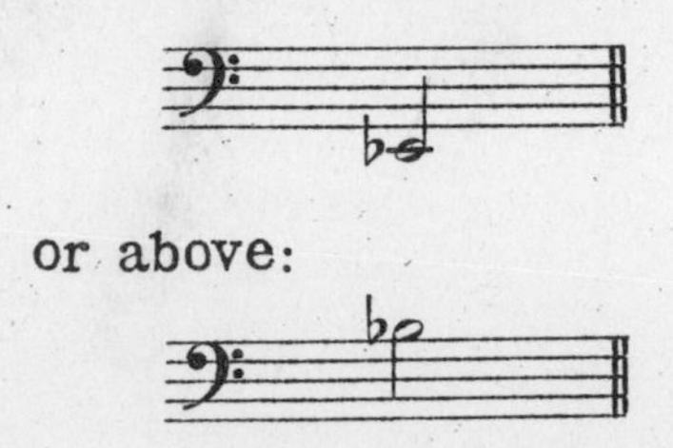

are difficult and should not be written, for the reason that they require great expenditure of breath in the former and undue exertion in the latter case. Referring again to the fourth valve, it is more useful to facilitate difficult fingering than to extend the compass downward. The fourth valve generally has the same length of tubing as the 1st and 3rd combined and can be used to replace them in the same manner as the 3rd valve is used as a substitute for the 1st and 2nd. Also, where the 1st, 2nd and 3rd valves are required in combination, the 2nd and 4th answer the purpose, and so on.

The BB flat bass with three valves covers a chromatic compass of two octaves and a diminished fifth as is usual with all three valved brass instruments, viz:

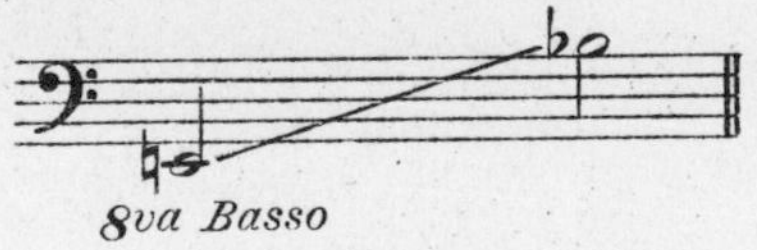

The extreme low notes on the BB flat bass require time for their production and should not be written in march music. Rapid passages below:

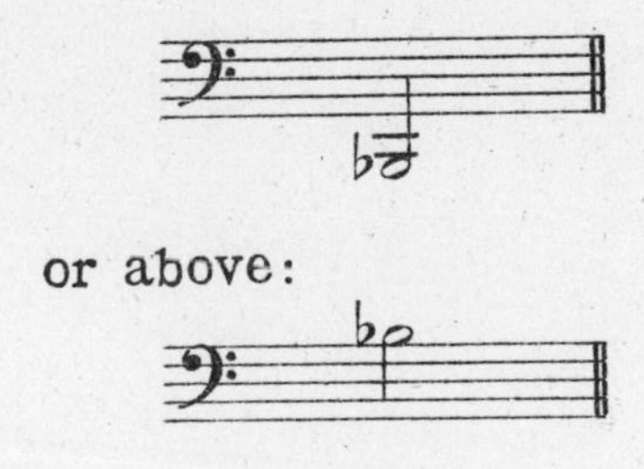

are precarious, and should not be written for reasons already given in the paragraph respecting the E flat bass.

Trills, double tonguing, etc., while possible, should be avoided unless some special effect is desired.

To sum up, the amalgamated compass of the brass bass section of our American bands gives the following extensive range:

almost identical with that of the four stringed contra-bass.

NOTE:- In small bands, where only one bass is used, the BB flat should be given preference over the E flat for the reason that the low tones come out fuller and better on the BB flat Bass. The high notes are also easier to produce on the latter instrument.

THE STRING BASS

The Double-Bass, or Contra-Bass, is the largest in size and deepest in pitch of all stringed instruments played with the bow. It has a practical compass of two octaves and a perfect fourth, viz:

and sounding an octave lower.

The double-bass is frequently used for concert work in large Military Bands. The effect produced by the string element, employed in this capacity, is that of lightness and smoothness. In staccato passages for brass and reed basses the addition of one or two string basses playing pizzicato is very effective.

The double-bass blends well with all bass wind instruments, reed and brass; it softens and rounds out to a marked degree the tone quality of the entire bass section.

PERCUSSION

Percussion instruments are divided into two general classes, (1) those of definable pitch, and (2) those of indefinable pitch. The former class consists of the following: Bells (bars and tubular,) chimes, tympani, xylophones, etc. (modern bells and xylophones are equipped with resonators, the purpose of which is to amplify the fundamental tone, thereby subduing to some extent the upper partials, or harmonics, and thus giving due prominence to the fundamental tone.) Class (2) consists of snare and bass drum, tambourines, cymbals, triangle, castanets, etc.

All drums; tympani, bass and snare drums, may be described as resonance chambers covered with a stretched disc of elastic parchment struck with a stick.

The bass and snare drums are equipped with two heads or discs; one of heavier material than the other, is known as the batter head. The tympani is fitted with a single head adjusted by means of set screws around its circumference. The membrane being stretched over a metal basin, which acts as an amplifier, gives forth a sound of definable pitch.

Other paraphernalia, known as drummers' traps, may be classified under the heading of percussion. Traps consist of the following: bird whistles (assorted), baby cry, cow bawl, cow bell, cuckoo imitation, siren, tom-toms, wood block, chinese drum, train and steamboat whistles (these latter sound three different pitches simultaneously), sleigh bells, train imitation, anvils, etc.

Percussion Instruments of Definable Pitch

TYMPANI

The Tympani, or kettle drums, are the most important and effective of the percussion instruments. Parts for them are notated in the bass clef and sound as written. A pair of tympani, varying slightly in size, are used in the military band. Their chief function, in former times, was to reinforce the tonic and dominant of the key to which they were tuned. Also, they were used occasionally on the tonic and subdominant. A more independent use and treatment of the tympani began with Beethoven and the later composers. They are now tuned to such intervals as major and minor seconds, thirds, sixths, sevenths, and perfect fourths, fifths and octaves, according to requirement. The large tympani can be tuned to any of the following notes:

and the small one to:

The notes marked (x) are not considered good for the reason that the lowermost note on the large drum is dull and the higher ones on both drums have little tone due to excessive stretching of the membranes (heads).

All kinds of rhythmical figures, rolls, tremolos, etc., can be performed with ease on the tympani. Their character expresses itself in their power of concussion. From ***ppp*** to ***fff*** is possible, with every degree of shading between these two extremes. They are useful in almost every variety of musical composition. In dramatic music, funeral marches and storm scenes they particularly excel.

The simultaneous use of both tympani, shown in the following illustration, is always effective but should be used with discretion.

These double parts should be used only to mark rhythmical figures and not for the purpose of a double roll effect by one player, viz:

This style, at the best, is effective only when numerous other instruments are playing *f* or *ff* The effect is always better when the player uses only one drum.

The roll or tremolo is written for tympani as follows:

Rolls of varied lengths, used in conjunction with other rhythmical figures, are:

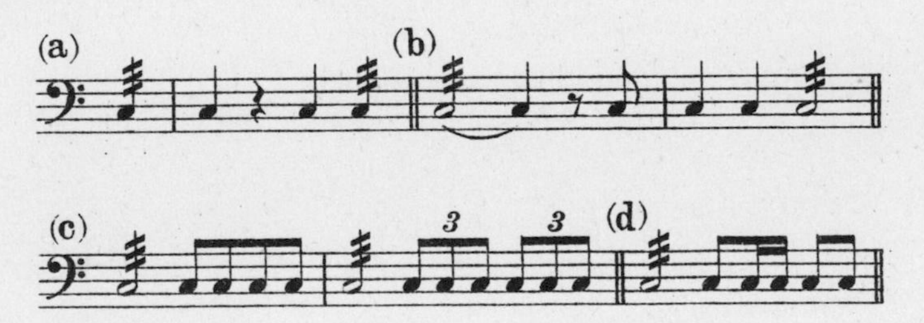

The tonal quality of both tympani in *pp* and *ppp* is mysterious in character. In *f* and *ff* it becomes powerful and stirring. All varieties of nuance and dynamics are possible and effective. Two kinds of sticks are used for tympani playing; one set with soft sponge-like heads for the performance of light *p* and *pp* passages, and the other of felt for *f* and *ff* playing. Tympani may also be used muted or muffled in requiems and sad scenes. This is made possible by covering the heads with a cloth.

The difficulty of rapid changing in tuning, which obtains in modern music has been greatly modified by the invention of the pedal tympani or machine drum. While this invention has not as yet come into general use, the mechanism has been perfected by American manufacturers and the pedal tympani is now used with great success by many of the best tympanists. Each tympani is equipped with a pedal attachment which may be tightened or slackened at will, thereby changing the pitch. By means of apparatus fixed into the upper frame of the tympani, the player can attend to the various tunings beforehand and not be obliged to test by tapping during the performance, as required on the ordinary tympani when a change of tuning is desired. The pedals of the tympani when depressed makes readily available the following notes:

Until the pedal tympani comes into general use, it would seem that composers and arrangers should avoid, as much as possible, rapid changes of key during the performance of a piece.

ORCHESTRA or BAR BELLS

Orchestra or Bar Bells have a chromatic compass of about two octaves, written from middle C to two octaves above, and sounding an octave higher than the written notes. As a rule, the signature of a key is not given in bell parts, the accidentals being placed before the notes as required. Rapid rhythmical figures are not often written for bells. Diatonic or chromatic progressions are possible and good upon them, and may be played rapidly or slowly, according to the skill of the player.

Due to the prominence of their overtones, bar bells do not sound well when two are played simultaneously in harmony, although in certain classes of music (chiefly descriptive) they are so scored for.

In the military band, bell parts are played by the drummers. The parts being written with those for the drums.

Good examples of the bells' usefulness may be found in the Overture "If I Were King" by Adam, "Prelude" by Jarnefeldt, and "Aus aller Herren Länder" by Moskowski.

Heavy tubular bells, or chimes, such as are used in Tschaikowsky's "Overture 1812," are in general use. These large bells are well suited to music of a religious character as well as for pastoral scenes. Meyerbeer in "The Huguenots," Rossini in "William Tell," Verdi in "Il Trovatore," and Wagner in "Parsifal" have employed large bells with wonderful results.

THE XYLOPHONE

The Xylophone consists of a number of semi-circular pieces of wood of varied sizes, arranged in order on, and bound by, two strings; these are laid on two straws or tubes in such a way that each bar is disconnected from the other, and are sounded by a pair of small wooden hammers. Parts for them are written in the treble clef and sound an octave higher than written.

Their compass is approximately:

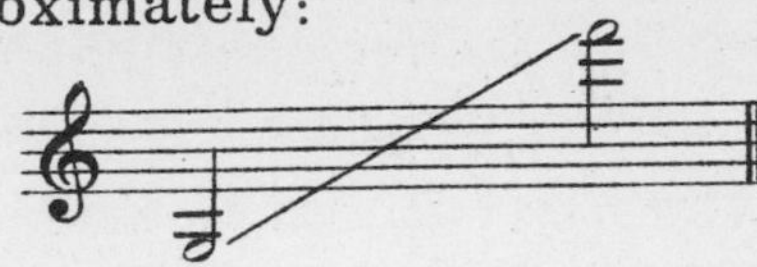

with all chromatic intervals.

In the hands of a skillful player, nearly all rhythmical figures, passages, and ornaments are playable upon the xylophone.

This instrument is used chiefly for solos and dance, or descriptive music. Saint-Saens has used it very effectively in his "Danse Macabre," to imitate the sound of the rattling bones of a skeleton.

THE ANVIL

Anvils of varying sizes, tuned in several ways, are used to some extent in military bands. While they cannot be called tuneful instruments they are nevertheless of definable pitch. As a rule they are employed in pairs, tuned in minor thirds, viz:

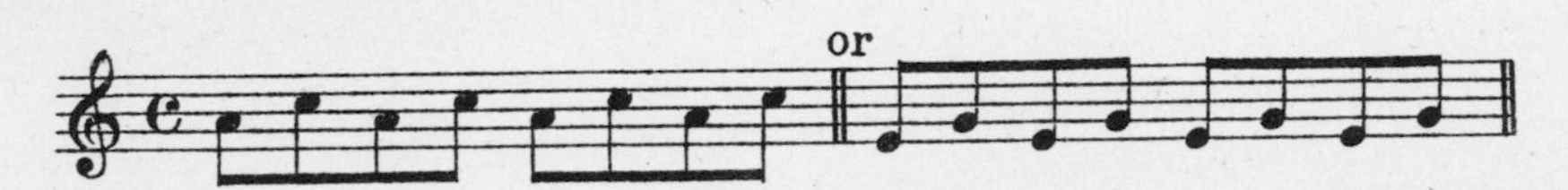

For characteristic purposes they are very effective and useful. Verdi used them in his "Il Trovatore," and Wagner in "Siegfried" and "Rheingold."

Percussion Instruments of Indefinable Pitch

THE SNARE DRUM

The Snare Drum, called also "military drum," has a clear and rattling sound, due to the snares of gut stretched across the lower head or membrane. While employed quite frequently in modern orchestra scores, its true sphere is in the military band. In music of a martial character it particularly excels. It is also well adapted for use in dance music. While the chief use of this drum is to reinforce rhythms, the most varied and complicated figures are playable upon it by means of two sticks. Similarly with the tympani; tremolos, rolls, etc., in all grades of power from *ppp* to *fff* are possible on the snare drum. The manner of writing for it is here illustrated:

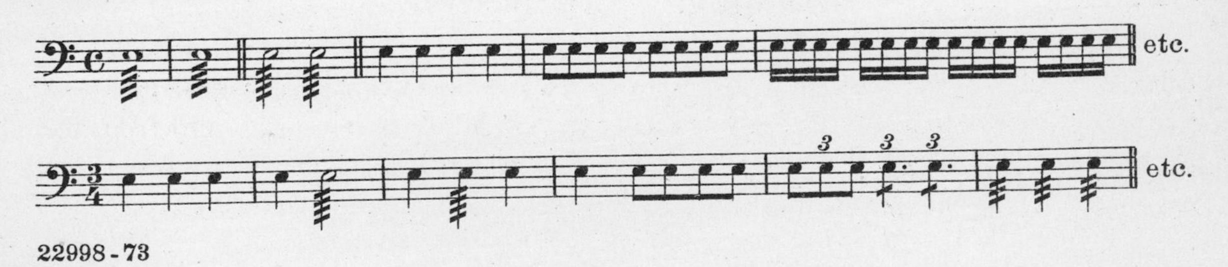

The usefulness of the snare drum may best be described in the following classified manner, (1) for accompanying:

(2) to support the rhythm:

and (3) to support the melody rhythmically:

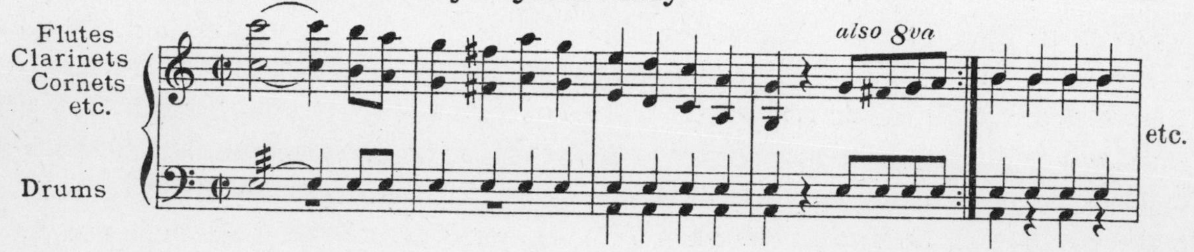

Frequently, snare drum and bass drum parts are written together, especially in American band arrangements. Music for triangle, bells and other percussion instruments (traps) are also often included in the drum parts; the name of the instrument required being written over the part.

The snare drum may be muted, or muffled, by making the snares slack, thereby checking the vibrations. Muted effects are useful in certain classes of descriptive music (oriental and the like). They are also used for funeral marches.

THE BASS DRUM

The Bass Drum is used extensively in the military band, chiefly to mark the strong beats, reinforcing them with the basses; it may also be used to good advantage for characteristic purposes, viz., to imitate cannon shot, thunder, etc. In dance and military music it is indispensable. Bass drum parts are written as follows:

Bass Drum alone:

Bass and Snare Drum together:

A roll or tremolo may be produced on the bass drum with fine effect. It is written as follows:

The roll is produced by grasping the drum stick at its center, and, by means of a flexible wrist, striking the upper and lower ends of the drum with great rapidity. It is possible to play the roll in all degrees of power from *pp* to *ff*. The bass drum may be played with two sticks, one being held in each hand of the player. However, two sticks are not employed in American bands, nor are they necessary.

CYMBALS

Cymbals consist of two circular disks of metal with a hemispherical concavity in the center, on the outer side of which a strap is attached which serves as a holder. They are frequently employed in combination with the bass drum in small bands, that is, for concert work. On the march they are played separately. Much controversy between bandmasters exists as to the proper method of employing bass drum and cymbals. Some insist on having the cymbals attached to the bass drum, giving as a reason the necessity of both instruments being struck simultaneously. They also aver that by so doing the band saves the services of one player. Others assert that the usage of both instruments together are ruinous to the tone of cymbal and drum alike. It is believed that judicious employment of both methods are useful, depending of course on the class of music to be played. True enough the vibration of the cymbals is more or less damped when used in connection with the bass drum. However, for marches, overtures, and other musical compositions not of a descriptive character, it would seem that a more accurate rhythm could be secured by assigning both instruments to one player. Still, the true character of the cymbal and bass drum is lost entirely if they be employed unceasingly together. The strong metallic tone of the cymbal is much more satisfactory when they are played separately.

Swinging cymbals struck with the bass drum stick give forth tam-tam-like effects, but should only be employed in special and appropriate dramatic scenes, where they can be made exceedingly effective. The clang of cymbals is very penetrating, and in *mf* and *f* can be distinctly heard throughout the band. Cymbals are not solely instruments for noise making; they may be used with fine effect in *p* or *pp*, either with or without the bass drum. Gounod employed them in this manner in his "Gloria" (Cecilian Mass). Wagner in the "Tannhauser Overture" used them Forte without the bass drum, to depict the revels in the Venusberg.

CASTANETS

The Castanets (Spanish origin) are used in the orchestra and military band for rhythmical effects. They are chiefly used in ballet music or in musical compositions that require Spanish local color. Notation for them is shown in the following example:

Chabrier in his Rhapsody "España" used the castanets to good advantage. While parts for them are written much the same as for the snare drum, they are not required to produce the same amount of rhythmical variety.

THE TAMBOURINE

The Tambourine is very effective and useful in ballet music, gypsy scenes, and the like. Spaniards, Sicilians, and the inhabitants of the south of France make an extended use of it for their characteristic dances. Its notation is similar to that of the snare drums, but only with simple rhythm. Its use in the orchestra or band is rare, except in characteristic music of the natives of southern Europe. Weber in his "Preciosa," Donizetti in "Don Pasquale," David in "The Desert" and Bizet in the opera "Carmen" and his "L' Arlesienne" Suite No. 2, have used the tambourine very effectively.

THE TRIANGLE

As its name implies, this instrument is constructed of steel, bent into a triangular shape. It is caused to vibrate by means of a small steel rod and gives forth a great variety of tonal shadings, *p, pp, mf, f, ff;* crescendo and diminuendo can be produced upon it with fine effect. Its chief use is for decorative purposes, and when judiciously used it is capable of many and varied effects. Used indiscriminately the effect is trivial.

THE TAM-TAM

This instrument can be used to good advantage in scenes of horror, death, uncanniness or wild choruses. Its tone, when forcibly struck, is of a screaming, ear splitting variety. In *p* and *pp* it produces a mysterious, evil-boding quality of tone.

Its employment should be confined to depict only those scenes above enumerated.

Appendix to Part I

(a) REGISTER OF MUSICAL TONES

The location or register of tones are determined by dividing the GREAT STAFF into OCTAVE GROUPS as illustrated below:

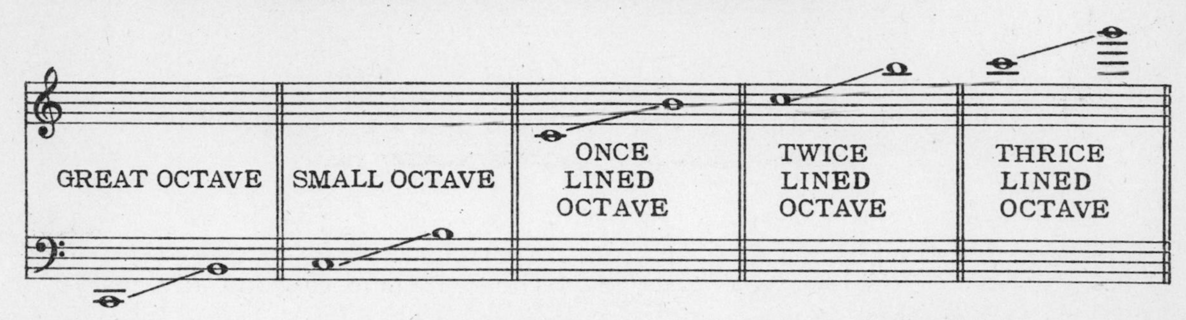

The meaning of the terms, ONCE LINED (a^1), TWICE LINED (c^2), GREAT (F), etc., are thus made apparent. The GREAT OCTAVE is expressed by Capital letters, viz:- G, A, B, etc; the SMALL OCTAVE by small letters d, e, f, etc; the ONCE LINED OCTAVE, the TWICE LINED OCTAVE, and the THRICE LINED OCTAVE by small letters with arabic numerals placed to the right of them; viz:- once lined c^1; twice lined c^2; and thrice lined c^3.

NOTE:- The DOUBLE GREAT or CONTRA OCTAVE sounding one octave lower than the GREAT is found complete only on the contra-bassoon and Pipe Organ, and nearly complete on the BB flat bass, E♭ Contra Bass sarrusophone and String Bass. The SUB-CONTRA OCTAVE sounding two octaves lower than the GREAT exists only on the largest Pipe Organs.

(b) SUMMARY CHART OF THE NOMINAL AND ACTUAL PITCH OF WIND INSTRUMENTS

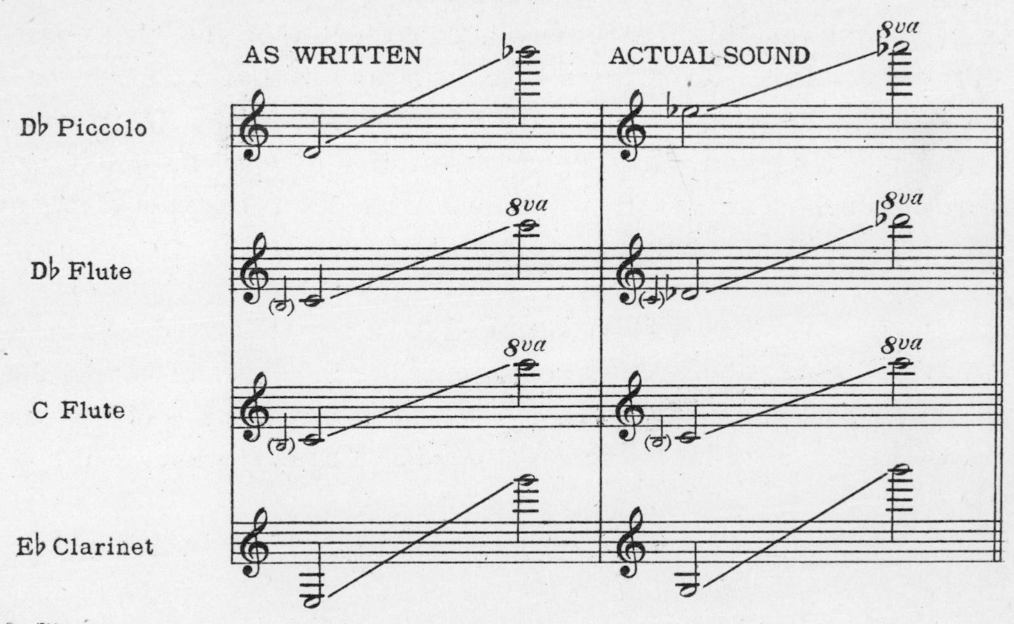

AS WRITTEN
ACTUAL SOUND
B♭ Clarinet
Alto Clarinet
Bass Clarinet
Oboe
8va
Bassoon
Contra Sarrusophone
8va
Basso
Soprano Saxophone
Alto Saxophone
C Melody Saxophone
Tenor Saxophone
Baritone Saxophone
Bass Saxophone
B♭ Cornet, Trumpet,
Flugelhorn

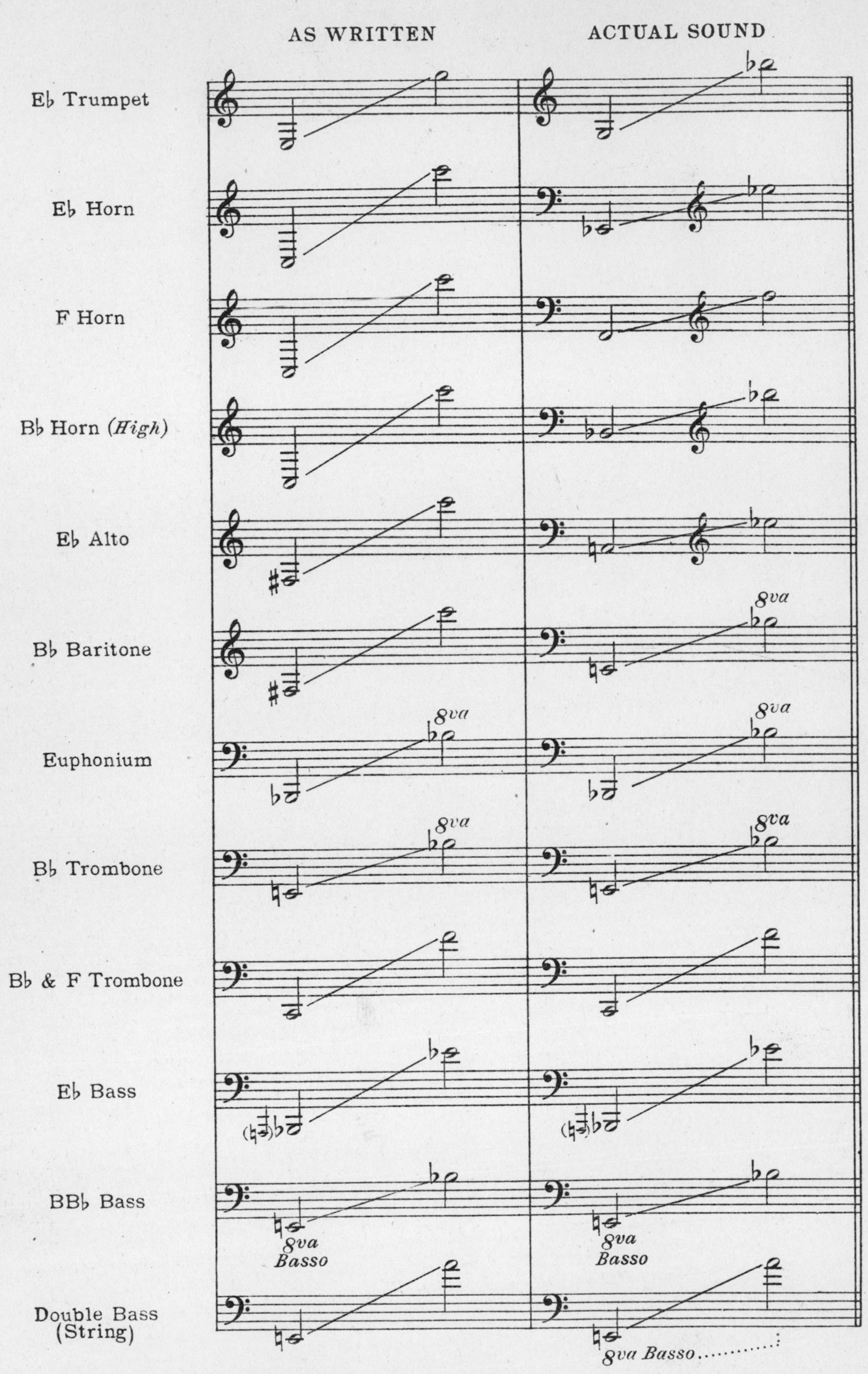

N.B. It is here recommended that the student provide himself with the "Carl Fischer, Inc. complete instrument chart"

PART TWO

MILITARY BAND ARRANGING

The arrangement of music for military band, if it be done in an artistic manner, requires five essentials, viz: (1) a thorough knowledge of all the instruments used in the band (practical if possible); (2) skill in harmony, musical forms and elementary counterpoint; (3) keen judgment in combining the various choirs of instruments (reed and brass), and in the mixture of one family or choir with the other; (4) a theoretical knowledge of all organ stops, as well as the proper use of the piano pedal; (5) transposition.

Assiduous practice, combined with the knowledge already enumerated, is necessary if the arranger desires to become proficient in this important branch of military band study. The atrocious habit of throwing arrangements together perfunctorily, as the untrained are wont to do, cannot be too strongly condemned.

The system of band arranging adopted and practiced at the U. S. Army Music School is the outcome of years of careful study and much practical experience, and has been taught to the bandmaster students of that school since 1911 with excellent results. This system not only aims to equip the student with a knowledge of using all styles of composition suitable to the military band, but to present the subject in a classified and progressive manner.

There are five general classifications, viz: (1) arranging from hymn tunes (four-part harmony); (2) from choral music (part-songs, anthems, etc.); (3) from organ scores (concert pipe organ); (4) from orchestral scores, and (5) from piano solos. This latter class presents the greatest difficulty for the reason that the arranger must, in many cases, invent new parts, and considerable skill is necessary to do the work well.

CLASSIFICATION I - ARRANGING FROM HYMN TUNES

(a) Reed Quartets and Combinations

While the first lessons in band arranging must, as a necessity, be elementary, music of serious and dignified import should always be selected for the purpose. It is believed that hymn tunes afford the best examples for the reason that they are, as a rule, laid out in four-part harmony and are best suited to the student's first efforts, an explanation of which follows: The beginner should first make small arrangements, viz: quartets, double quartets, and small combinations, before attempting those for full band. (The selection of a good key for band must be carefully considered. Avoid sharp keys as much as possible). This practice has a fourfold purpose: (1) To acquaint the student with the various quartets and choirs of instruments used in the band; (2) to point out the good and bad registers used (best notes, etc.);

(3) to obtain a knowledge of balance among the different voices or instruments, and (4) to experiment with various combinations of instruments, whether they be single or double quartets of brass or reed, or mixed choirs of both reed and brass.

The following four measures of a well known hymn tune, which affords an ample illustration, may be treated in many ways, first as quartets for reed or brass, secondly as mixed combinations, and lastly for full band.

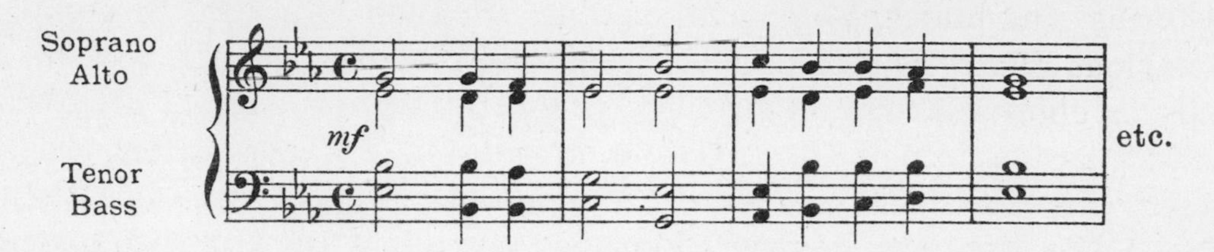

Two small arrangments, on the above exercise, designed to point out good and bad features, follow:

Number (1) of the foregoing is not considered a good arrangement for the reason that the flute part lies too low and would be overbalanced by the clarinets, the parts for which lie in the chalumeau register of those instruments. If the flute part were supplemented by a soprano saxophone the effect would be good.

Number (2,) a mixture of single and double reed, is an excellent arrangement; all notes on the various instruments lie in good registers and are of first-rate quality.

Other good reed quartets are: (a) Clarinet quartet (E flat, B flat, alto and bass, or two B flats, alto and bass.) (b) Double reed: two oboes and two bassoons (rather nasal; better when used in combination with other instruments). (c) Quartet of saxophones, soprano, alto, tenor, and baritone. (d) two oboes, B flat clarinet and bassoon. (e) Oboe, E flat clarinet, B flat clarinet, alto clarinet. (f) Mixtures of flute, single reed and double reed in quartets, single and double, as well as larger combinations.

When it is desired to strengthen weak sounding notes, or to soften the harsh sounding registers of the various instruments, it becomes necessary to seek the support of some other instrument, for example: The low (and weak) register of the flute may be doubled with good results by a B flat clarinet or soprano saxophone playing in unison. On the clarion register of the B flat clarinet (from twice lined C to its octave) the addition of a flute in unison has a softening effect. The flute will also soften those notes on the oboe. The "throat register" on the B flat clarinet (the weakest on the instrument) is greatly improved by a bassoon playing in unison. The lowermost register of the bassoon is more or less rough and may be greatly improved by the combination of a bass clarinet, in so far as its compass will permit, or the E flat contrabass sarrusophone.

To sum up, the weak registers of the various reed instruments, which were thoroughly explained in the first part of this work, should be well known to the arranger, and, whenever necessary in scoring, these weak registers should be supplemented by some other instrument.

An effective arrangement for flute and single and double reed, on the foregoing exercise, is herewith illustrated. A quartet of saxophones could be added with good results:

EXERCISE I

Make several reed arrangements patterned after illustrations and information given in Classification I (a) Reed Quartets and Combinations. Select material from any Church Hymnal or collection of hymns. Use an entire hymn for each exercise and, if possible, try them out with instruments in ensemble before passing on to the next lesson.

(b) Brass Quartets and Mixed Combinations

The brass choir of the military band comprises the following: (1) The trumpet family, consisting of trumpets and trombones; (2) the saxhorn or flugel family; (3) the cornet, and (4) the french horn. Illustrations on the same exercise, already given for the reeds, are here scored for brass instruments and mixtures of reed and brass:

Number (1). May be considered a good arrangement. All notes for the various instruments lie in the medium register. The tenor part may be played by a trombone with good results. A mixture of the saxhorns and trumpet family would then exist. In order to secure a proper balance in this quartet the baritone and euphonium parts should be played softly.

Number (2). An excellent arrangement. The flugelhorn parts may be played by cornets if desired.

Other good quartets for brass instruments follow:

(a) Two B♭ trumpets and two B♭ trombones (trumpet family).

(b) Two B♭ cornets and two B♭ trombones (mixture of saxhorns and trumpets).

(c) Two B♭ trumpets, baritone and euphonium (mixture of saxhorns and trumpets).

(d) Quartet of french horns. In a quartet arrangement for horns it is well to employ F horns on the two upper voices to avoid high notes which are difficult for the ordinary player. The E♭ horns may play the tenor and bass parts. However, in full band arrangements of hymn tunes it is quite unlikely that the horns will cover all four parts; a more practical way of scoring would be to allot the inner parts (alto and tenor) to them, the first and second horn playing the alto part and the third and fourth the tenor part.

(e) B♭ cornet, first and second E♭ altos and baritone. This is only a fair arrangement. The two altos on the inner parts would have a tendency to make the quartet sound dull.

(f) Two french horns in F and two B♭ trombones. (A splendid quartet).

(c) Mixtures for Reed and Brass Instruments

Two excellent quartets, one a mixture of saxhorns and saxophones, and the other for french horns and saxophones, follow:

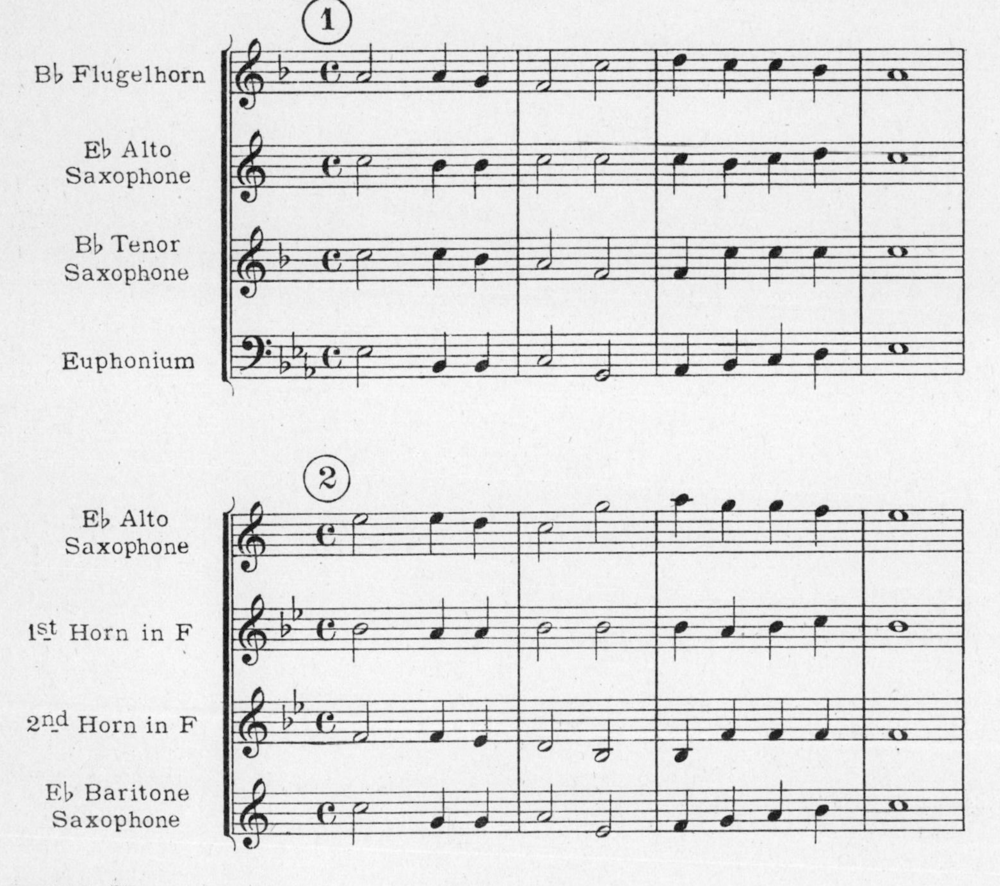

Another arrangement for french horns and saxophones may be made as follows: Alto saxophone on the soprano part, first horn in F on the alto, tenor saxophone on the tenor, and second horn in E♭ on the bass part. This quartet would be good provided the second horn part (which lies rather low) be performed by a first-rate player.

An effective arrangement for brass instruments and saxophones may be scored as follows: (the various parts; soprano, alto, tenor and bass being played by the instruments enumerated under each heading)

Soprano Part

Solo B♭ Cornet
Solo B♭ Trumpet
First B♭ Cornet
First B♭ Trumpet
Soprano Saxophone

Alto Part

Second B♭ Cornet
Second B♭ Trumpet
First Horn or Alto
Alto Saxophone
Flugelhorn in B♭

Tenor Part

Baritone
Trombones 1st and 2nd
Second Horn or Alto
Tenor Saxophone

Bass Part

Euphonium
Bass Trombone
E♭ Bass
BB♭ Bass
Baritone Saxophone

EXERCISE II

Make several brass arrangements and mixed arrangements of brass and reeds (saxophones) patterned after illustrations and information given in Classification I (b) and (c). Select material as suggested in Exercise I and carry out instructions as there noted.

(d) Full Band Arrangement

The difference in the treatment of wind instruments in quartet and small arrangements, as compared with one for full band, will become readily apparent when the following full score is compared with the small combinations already given:

A careful analysis of this score illustrates how a simple four-part hymn may be distributed for band. Many changes are, of course, possible; for example, when the melody (soprano part) lies too high to be played 8va by the solo and 1st B♭ clarinets (it does not in this arrangement) the 2nd clarinet may play the melody as written; the 1st and 3rd clarinets playing the alto and tenor parts in the upper octave; the 1st baritone may play the melody 8va Basso, if desired; the inner parts (alto and tenor) may be allotted to the bassoons, and the melody to the alto saxophone, etc.

EXERCISE III

Select four or five *different* hymn tunes, from material such as suggested in Exercise I, and arrange each for full band conformable with the model and instruction given in Classification I (d.) Try them out with a full band if possible.

CLASSIFICATION II-ARRANGING FROM CHORAL MUSIC

The arranging of choral music (part songs, anthems, etc.) for military band will now be considered. As already stated, the selection of a good key for military band should be given careful consideration, those with flat signatures being the most practical.

The vocal parts are, as a rule, allotted to a brass quartet, for example: Two trumpets and two trombones, or, two trumpets (or cornets) trombone and euphonium, or two flugelhorns (or cornets) E♭ alto and euphonium, depending on the nature of the composition and the effect desired. (reference to the various quartets and combinations of reed and brass instruments, previously noted, is here recommended). A single brass quartet may be supplemented by a quartet of saxophones with fine effect. Accompanying parts are scored for the remaining instruments; the same being arranged in the manner already prescribed for hymn tunes.

Four measures of a vocal number (mixed quartet) with accompaniment, is here given with a full band arrangement of it.

The Belfry Tower

HATTON

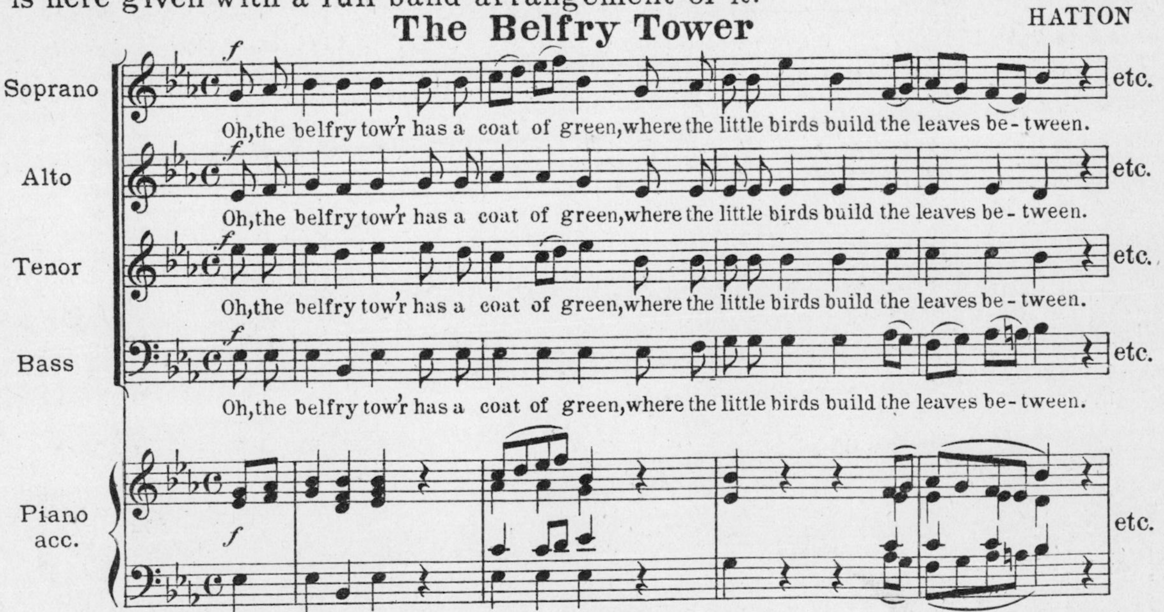

The Belfry Tower
HATTON-WHITE
47
Flutes
Oboes
E♭Clarinet
Solo & 1st B♭Clarinets 2nd & 3rd
Alto Clarinet
Bass Clarinet
Saxophones
Soprano
Alto
Tenor
Baritone
VOICE PARTS
Bassoons
Solo & 1st B♭Cornets 2nd & 3rd
Trumpets
Trombones
1st & 2nd E♭Horns (Altos) 3rd & 4th
Baritones
1st & 2nd Trombones 3rd
Basses (Tubas)
mf
etc.
8va Basso
Drums (Tacet)
22998-73

Many diversions from this example may be made, depending on the character of the vocal selection to be arranged. Anthems, part songs, etc., are frequently interspersed with solo or duet passages, with or without accompaniment, in which case treatment other than that illustrated becomes necessary. There are no hard and fast rules governing the arrangement of this, or any other style of composition.

Attention is here invited to the author's military band arrangement of the "Processional to Calvary" from the "Crucifixion," by Stainer. This work is published by Carl Fischer Inc. New York, and affords an example of varied scoring which is well worth reviewing.

EXERCISE IV

Select, at least four, mixed vocal quartets with piano accompaniment and arrange each for full band, first with two trumpets and two trombones playing the vocal parts; secondly, with a mixed brass quartet (2 cornets or flugelhorns, E♭ alto and euphonium) playing the vocal parts; thirdly, with two B♭ cornets and two trombones playing the vocal parts, and lastly, with a mixture of saxophones and brass (double quartet) carrying the vocal parts. This latter arrangement to conform with the model given under Classification II. Try them out with a full band if possible.

CLASSIFICATION III

Arranging from Organ Scores

Organ scores offer the student of band arranging better material than any other style of composition, for the reason that many of the varieties of tone color existing in the organ are paralleled in the military band. Moreover, a similarity of tone exists between the organ and wind instruments (particularly the wood-winds and large reeds). Therefore, in order to make creditable arrangements from organ scores, it is necessary for the student to have some knowledge of the organ and its various "stops," which often give forth sounds very different in pitch to the written note. A "stop" controls several "pipes" (the acoustic principle of pipes are both "stopped" and "open"). The pipes are divided into two principal groups, (1) Flue-pipes and (2) Reed-pipes. They may be conical, cylindrical, or rectangular in shape The tonal quality of the flue-pipes are sharp, bright, brilliant, dark, soft, tender, etc. The reed-pipes are classified as follows: (1) beating reeds, producing a hard blaring quality and (2), free reeds which are pleasing and bright in tone. Stopped pipes give forth sounds an octave lower than open pipes of the same length, but their quality of tone in more subdued. Stopped pipes are referred to as 4-foot tone, 8-foot tone, etc., whereas open pipes are called 4-foot length, 8-foot length, etc.

Organ stops are divided (broadly) into (1) Plain and (2) Mixture stops.

A different species are the *Mutation stops.* They control pipes, each note of which is accompanied by overtones produced from small pipes. These overtones provide enriching harmonic elements. They are the *Quint, Tierce, Twelfth, Sesquialtera of three ranks,* and the *Mixture of three ranks.* When great C is sounded these stops will give forth sounds as follows:

Mixture stops are sometimes known by the generic name of Compound stops, because they are compounded of two or more ranks of pipes, of various pitches. In order to fully understand the exact range and tonal qualities of the various organ stops, the student should provide himself with a Dictionary of Organ Stops and study it carefully. It is important that the definitions of the following stops be looked up: Foundation stop, Mutation stop, Mixtures, Sesquialtera. The "Dictionary of Organ Stops," by J. I. Wedgewood (G. Schirmer, New York), is recommended as a reference book.

The organ is equipped with two keyboards called (1) Manual and (2) Pedal. Large organs are built with 4 or 5 manuals placed step-wise one above the other. The manuals are operated by the hands, and the 'Pedal' the foot.

The manuals control: The Great Organ, the Swell Organ, the Choir Organ and the Echo Organ. The pedals: The Pedal Organ.

The Wind Band parallel to the great organ would be the full military band: to the swell organ; all reeds and light brass: to the choir and echo organ; reeds (without the baritone and bass saxophones) and french horns. The euphonium would suffice for bass.

The manuals have a chromatic compass of about $4\frac{1}{2}$ octaves (54 keys in chromatic succession), written:

and the Pedals about two octaves, written:

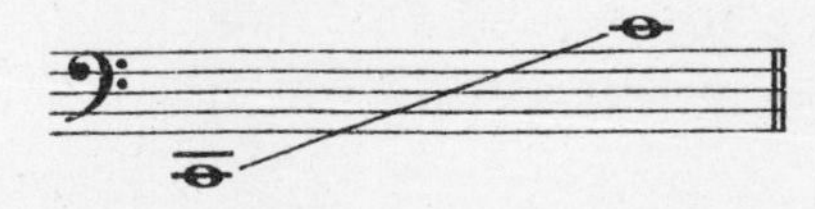

The complete tonal compass of the organ (although written from great C to thrice lined F), will give forth the following sounds:

Sounds 2 octaves lower	Sounds one octave lower	Sounds as written	Sounds 8va	Sounds 2 octaves higher
32 FOOT	16 FOOT	8 FOOT	4 FOOT	2 FOOT

The band arranger must therefore consider that organ pipes of different lengths sound as follows: 2-foot pipes two octaves higher than written; 4-foot pipes one octave higher than written; 8-foot pipes as written; 16-foot pipes one octave lower than written; and 32-foot pipes two octaves lower than written.

Indications of lengths of pipes involved are almost invariably written at the beginning of a composition for organ. For example:

Registration Great: Full organ to swell.
" Swell: 16 ft., 8 ft., and 4 ft., work, no reeds.
" Choir: Flutes 8 ft. and 4 ft.
" Pedal: Full, coupled to great, etc.

The four opening bars of the "GRAND CHORUS IN B♭" for organ by Th. Dubois (see illustration), indicates that the great organ is employed.

"Grand Chorus in B♭"

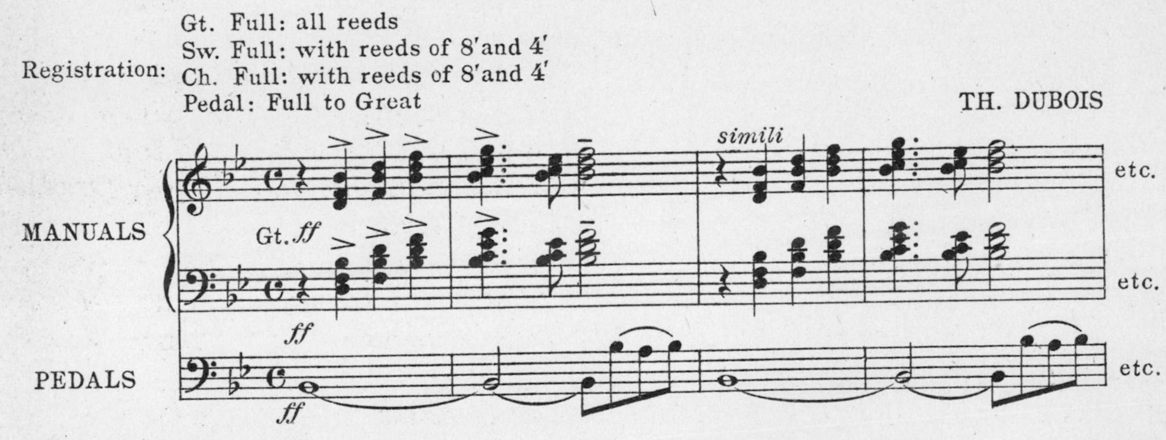

Its parallel, then, would require the resources of the full military band. The sign (Gt., meaning Great Organ) implies that all stops, 2 ft., 4 ft., 8 ft., 16 ft., and 32 ft., are employed. This requires the doubling of manual parts in octaves (viz.: one octave, and two octaves higher than written). The Pedals, an octave lower, and, wherever practicable, two octaves lower than written.

The following example, arranged for full military band, illustrates the foregoing four measures of the "GRAND CHORUS IN B♭."

"Grand Chorus in B♭"
TH. DUBOIS-WHITE
Piccolo
Flutes
Oboes
E♭ Clarinets
Solo & 1st B♭ Clarinets 2nd & 3rd
Alto Clarinet
Bass Clarinet
Saxophones
Soprano
Alto
Tenor
Baritone
Bassoons
Solo & 1st B♭ Cornets 2nd & 3rd
1st & 2nd E♭ Horns (Altos) 3rd & 4th
Baritones
Trombones
Basses (Tubas)
Tympani in B♭ & F
ff
sempre
etc.

NOTE: (A full military band arrangement of this excellent organ composition-"GRAND CHORUS IN B♭" by Dubois - is published by Carl Fischer, Inc. New York, and contains a variety of scoring which will well repay a careful review by the student).

Scoring for smaller combinations of wind instruments to parallel the "Swell" and "Choir Organ," which are really components of the Great Organ, will now be considered.

As previously stated, the wind band parallel to the Swell Organ would, as a general rule, include all reeds, flute, and light brass, viz: Flute, oboe, bassoon, all clarinets (E♭, B♭, Alto, and Bass), Alto, Tenor, and Baritone saxophones, cornets, flugelhorns, french horns and euphonium. It is not always necessary, nor desirable, to use all instruments in a continuous tutti, when scoring from the Swell Organ part, but a judicious selection should be made from among them and care taken not to overload the score. Careful study of the registers of the "Stops" should be made. As before noted, the 2-foot stops will sound two octaves higher, 4 - foot stops one octave higher, 8 - foot stops as written, 16 - foot stops one octave lower, and 32-foot stops two octaves lower than written in the organ score.

The Choir Organ could be paralleled with the following instruments: Flute and all reeds, except the Tenor, Baritone and Bass saxophones. One flugelhorn or cornet, two french horns and one euphonium. Similarly with the instructions given for the Swell Organ instrumentation, care should be taken not to score too heavily.

The accompanying extract from Gluck's "Orpheus" Ballet No. 18, written for the Choir Organ (8 ft. stops), is arranged for 4 B♭ clarinets, alto clarinet, bass clarinet, french horn and bassoon.

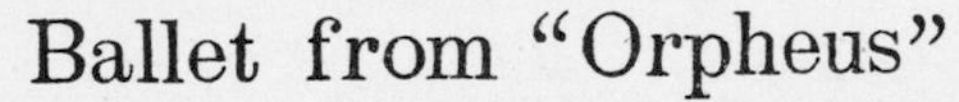

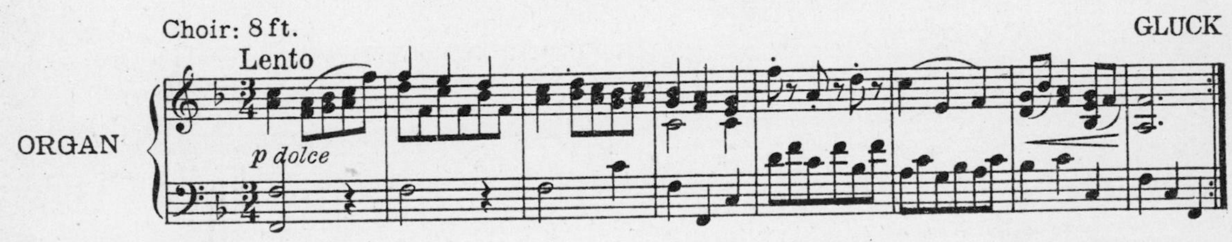

Wind Instrument arrangement of the extract from Ballet (ORPHEUS)

GLUCK - WHITE

The second part of the ballet, immediately following this extract, would require the use of a flute and oboe, and perhaps a cornet or flugelhorn.

In conclusion, it may be well to mention the fact that to arrange well from organ scores, or any other for that matter, the student must experiment considerably with passages requiring only a few instruments to record them and remember that the greater the variety of tonal-types used in combination, the greater will be the wealth and beauty of tonal shadings. Therefore, a band should always be available for the use of the student, that he might hear his work played. It is often necessary to "cue" passages where a mixture of certain brass and reed instruments are needed, in order that a careful selection of the best sounding combination may be made after the tryout with the band. There are no set rules for the student arranger to follow. Work, continuous and incessant, if he have sufficient theoretical foundation to carry it forward, will alone bring results. The arranger should practice as diligently with his pen as the successful performer must with his instrument.

EXERCISE V

Select not less than four organ compositions (preferably from the list given below) and arrange each for full band conformable with the instruction given under Classification III. Try them out with full band if possible.

N.B. The following list of organ music is recommended to the student for arranging material. There are many others published in folio form by Carl Fischer, Inc. N.Y.

Grand Chorus . . Alex Guilmant. . Op. 52, No. 2
Bridal Chorus. . Alex Guilmant. . Op. 58, No. 2
Scherzo Symphonique. . Alex Guilmant. . Op. 55, No. 2
Offertoire in A♭ Major. . Batiste
Offertoire in G Major. . Batiste
Album of Marches for Organ. . Scotson Clark
Album of "Twelve Pieces" for Organ. . Th. Dubois

CLASSIFICATION IV
ARRANGING FROM ORCHESTRAL SCORES

Arranging from orchestra scores involves less inventive ability than arranging from vocal scores, organ scores, or piano music, but a more thorough knowledge of wind instruments is necessary, for the reason that, while string performers can play for a great length of time without rest, the reverse is true of wind instrumentalists. Breathing places; the best notes on the practical registers of wind instruments; and the overlapping of the various register of individual families or choirs of wind instruments must be considered (see Part I). Moreover, strict attention to making a good parallel to the orchestra with respect to tonal balance, variety of tone color, etc., must be given.

A table showing two ways in which the orchestra parts may be paralleled by the military band follows:

(ORCHESTRA)	(WIND BAND PARALLELS) (1)	(2)
Flutes	Flute and Oboe	Flute and E♭ Clarinet
Oboes	Trumpets	Oboe and Soprano Saxophone
Clarinets	Cornets	Saxophones
Bassoons	Trombones	Bassoon and Baritone Saxophone
Horns	Saxophones	Horns
Trumpets	Trumpets	Trumpets
Trombones	Trombone and Euphonium	Trombones
Tympani	Tympani	Tympani
Drums	Drums	Drums
1st Violins	Solo and 1st B♭ Clarinets	Solo and 1st B♭ Clarinets
2nd Violins	2nd and 3rd B♭ Clarinets	2nd and 3rd B♭ Clarinets
Violas	Horns	Alto Clarinets
Cellos	Bass Clarinet and Bassoon	Bass Clarinet and Euphonium
Basses	Basses (Reed and Brass)	Basses (Reed and Brass)
Percussion	Percussion	Percussion

It is not always advisable nor desirable to adhere strictly to any one parallel between orchestra and band; for example, it is sometimes necessary, for the sake of tonal variety, to score the orchestra reed parts for brass instruments as the string parts are already being played by the military band reeds. Again, combinations of wind instruments as arranged in the orchestra score may be left unchanged when transcribed for band, or if more volume is required, they may be supplemented by other instruments. (See table of orchestra and wind band parallels).

The selection of a practical key for band must receive attention when arranging from orchestra scores; sharp keys being avoided as much as possible. Many of the technical difficulties possible for stringed instruments must be simplified when transcribed for band. A few illustrations covering the most important of these are given herewith:

Tremolos for the violins written:

are impossible for wind instruments and may be transcribed for the clarinets as follows:

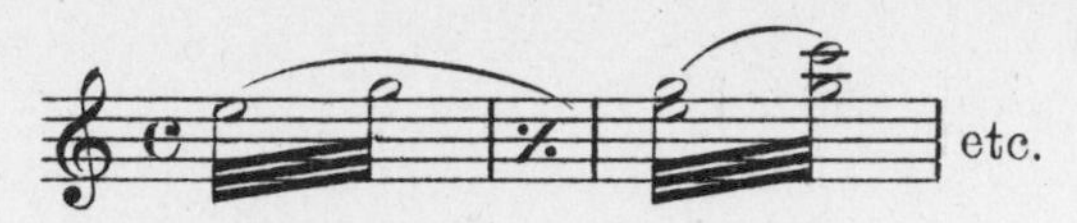

They then become easy and are very effective.

Another style of tremolo written:

may be transcribed in three ways for the clarinets, viz:

The first style is the most practical.

Reiterated notes, if they are required to be played in rapid tempo by the strings, should be simplified for the clarinets and written singly:

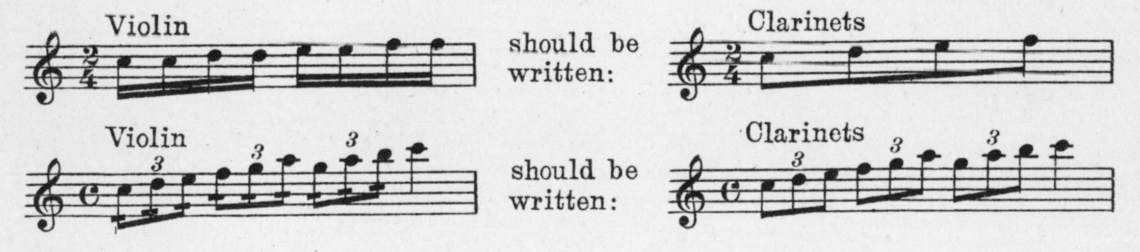

The string bass parts sound an octave lower than written, therefore, it becomes necessary to write them in the proper register for the brass and reed basses when scoring for band.

The following extract for string basses, which affords an ample illustration:

should be written for wind band basses as follows:

Pizzicato parts for the strings (first violins) may be written for clarinets as follows: (Single and double-stop illustrations are given).

Double stop pizzicato accompaniments for the 2nd Violins, Violas and Cellos of the orchestra, viz:

may be arranged for band as follows:

The double notes of the string pizzicato may be divided among separate players if desired. Still, the grace note effect, while more difficult to play, is the best imitation of the orchestra pizzicato. Violin chord pizzicato passages of more than two notes may be written for the clarinets by using the double acciacatura, viz:

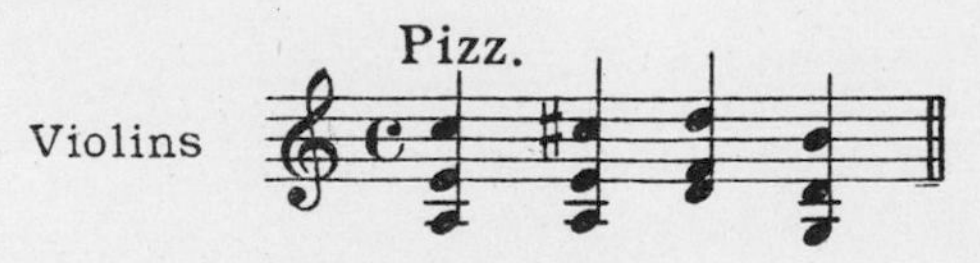

This style is applicable to slow tempo only. In MODERATO or ALLEGRO the principal notes, only, should be played staccato.

Arpeggios of the common chord variety are not difficult for the clarinets. However, the ascending and descending type, easily produced on the violin and viola in rapid tempo, are not so easy, and, to secure an effective performance of them, they should be distributed between two clarinets, the 2nd clarinet playing the first two ascending notes, also the last descending ones of the group in chords containing eight notes to a complete ascending and descending group. The 1st clarinet playing the upper notes in each case (see example):

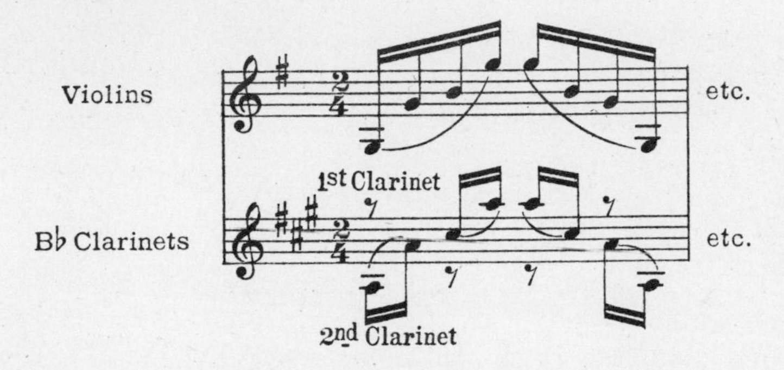

In the Triplet style, the 2nd clarinet may play the first and last note of each group as illustrated:

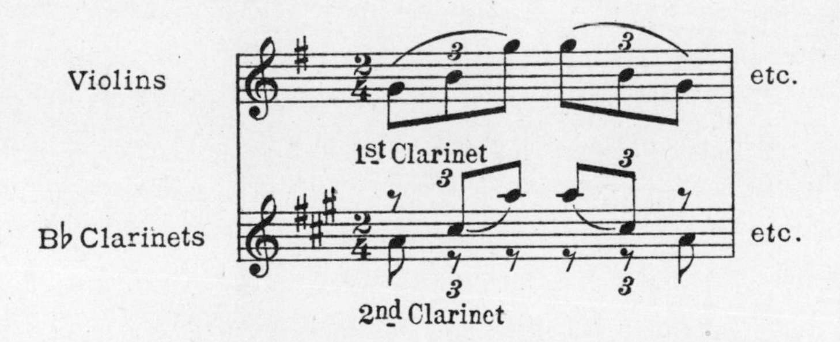

Muted passages for strings should be transcribed for the band reeds *ppp* in order to reduce as much as possible the intensity of sound. If brass is used it should be muted.

Harmonics for the strings, which of course differ in quality from the natural sounds, require tones in the high range of the band keyboard. The violin harmonics are best represented by flutes and piccolos; the viola harmonics by the E♭ clarinet, and the cello harmonics by the E♭ Alto clarinet or E♭ Alto saxophone. Passages so transcribed for band must be played *pp* and the accompaniment kept in the background, the brass being muted whenever practicable.

EXERCISE VI

Select several orchestra scores and transcribe them for full band, conformable with instruction given under Classification IV. The band parallels given in the table should be carefully adhered to. Try the arrangements with full band, if possible.

The following scores are recommended to the student for arranging material:

Album of Overtures	- Beethoven	(Peters Edition)
Album of Overtures	- Mendelssohn	(Peters Edition)
Album of Overtures	- Cherubini	(Peters Edition)
Symphonies 1 to 9	- Beethoven	(Peters Edition)
Italian Symphony	- Mendelssohn	(Peters Edition)
Scotch Symphony	- Mendelssohn	(Peters Edition)
Unfinished Symphony	- Schubert	(Peters Edition)
Symphonies 1 to 6	- Haydn	(Peters Edition)

(The Haydn Symphonies for small band arrangements)

NOTE:- Orchestra scores may be purchased from Carl Fischer Inc. New York.

CLASSIFICATION V
ARRANGING FROM PIANO MUSIC

Arranging for military band from piano music presents many and varied difficulties to the student. A good knowledge of harmony and elementary counterpoint is necessary, for the reason that ordinary piano solos are too thinly scored for the practical use of the arranger and it becomes necessary to invent new parts and also thicken (fill in) the harmony. The piano transcriptions of Liszt, the piano solos of Schumann, Rubinstein, Grainger and Rachmaninoff, do not, as a rule, require the invention of new parts or duplications in the chord structure, but it is often necessary in those compositions to thin out certain chords in close harmony that lie low on the band keyboard; otherwise a muddy effect will be produced, due to the fact that the upper partials, or harmonics, of such chords clash with disagreeable results. At this point it is recommended that the student review carefully the chapter on Consonances and Dissonances in "The Student's Helmholtz," by Broadhouse, also Chapter III on Acoustic Knowledge in "The Principles of Wind-Band Transcription." Clappe [Carl Fischer, Inc. New York].

Another difficulty in making band arrangements from piano music, is to give as nearly as possible an exact reproduction of the composer's meaning; sometimes it is impossible to do so and can only be approximated.

The selection of a good key for band is, of course, necessary. Sharp keys being avoided as much as possible. The piano music to be arranged should first be studied at the piano keyboard and the added parts penciled in.

As the piano lacks in sustaining power, the composer of piano music often finds it necessary to use a legato tremolo in order to produce sustained effects. Thus:

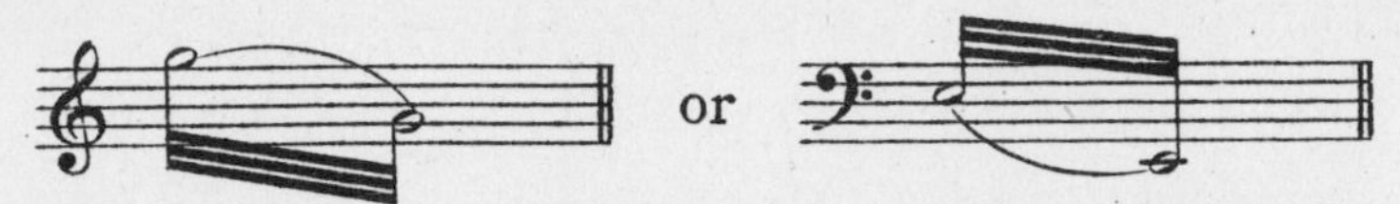

Such passages, when arranged for band, should be written as plain sustained notes, or, if the character of the composition demands it, in reiterated form. For example, a tremolo written for the piano like the following:

may be scored for the basses and bass trombone, as follows:

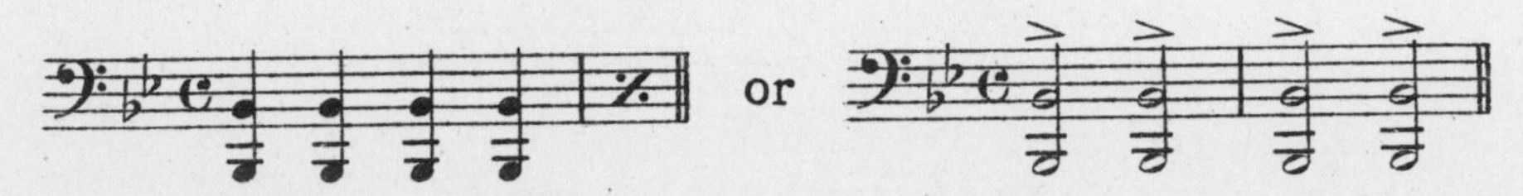

In addition to which, the E♭ french horns may be used with fine effect on sustained notes in the upper octaves, viz:

Passages for piano, that are required to be sustained are also indicated by the word Pedal, abbreviated (Ped.). The discontinuance of the use of the Pedal is indicated by the sign (❋) viz: (Ped. ❋). The use of the pedal must therefore be carefully watched by the arranger and passages so marked should be written out for wind instruments, for example:

could be transcribed for band as follows:

Octave skips for piano (left hand, bass part) may be reproduced without change by the bassoons and Baritone saxophone in moderato tempo; the basses and Bass trombone playing only the first note of the figure, for example:

Piano etc.

Bassoons and Baritone saxophone playing as written and basses and Bass trombone as follows:

Skips of an octave in the right hand (upper part) for piano would sound well if arranged for band as follows:

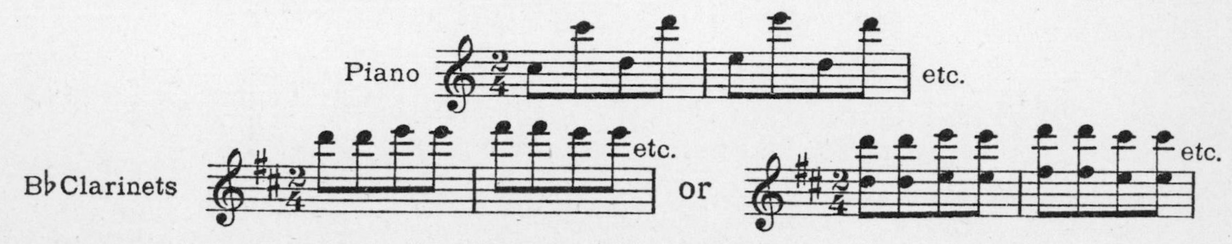

Accompaniments for the left hand (piano) viz:

are transcribed for the band in various ways. An example, showing the most practical way of arranging a simple piano accompaniment for band is here given:

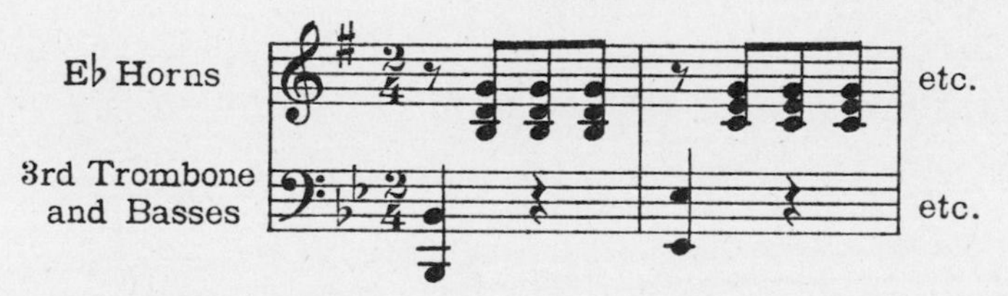

The 1st and 2nd trombones may, in such accompaniments, play the proper chord on the beat with the basses, or, if desired, sustained tones or counter melodies may be written for them. As already stated a great many piano arrangements require added parts to make them suitable for band transcriptions; added parts, however, should conform strictly to the already existing harmony. No attempts to deviate from the original work of the composer should be made. The student is again cautioned against the overloading of the various voices, or parts, by excessive "filling in," thus destroying the character of the composition which he is arranging.

Tremolos written for the right hand may either be played as sustained notes or arranged for the clarinets in the various ways already illustrated in Classification IV where transcription of the tremolo from orchestra violin parts for the clarinets is noted.

In order to recapitulate what has already been explained, in reference to the tremolo for piano and its application to military band instruments, an extract from the piano score of the opera "Ruddigore" by Sullivan is illustrated herewith, together with an arrangement of it for military band:

"Extract from Ruddigore"

SIR ARTHUR SULLIVAN

Piano arpeggios may be treated as a series of simple chords when arranged for band, or, if the tempo be not too rapid, they may be written in the form of a **gruppetto** preceding the principal note; analogous to the transcription of chords for the clarinets (See Classification IV). The effect of this latter style is very brilliant, viz:

The same arranged for B♭ clarinets

The foregoing **gruppetto** effect can only be played by the clarinets or flutes; brass instruments, saxophones **and oboes, should play the simple** notes, semi-staccato.

The following extract from Schulhoff's "Valse Brilliante" will serve as an example of adding parts in a piano composition selected for arranging purposes. The melody would, of course, be written an octave higher for flutes, E♭ and Solo B♭ clarinets when scored for full band.

Extract from "Valse Brillante"

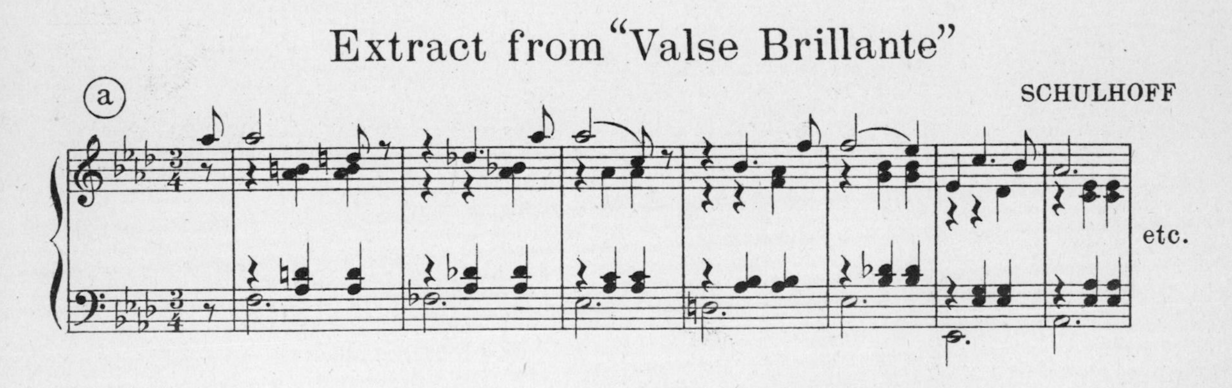

The same with added parts

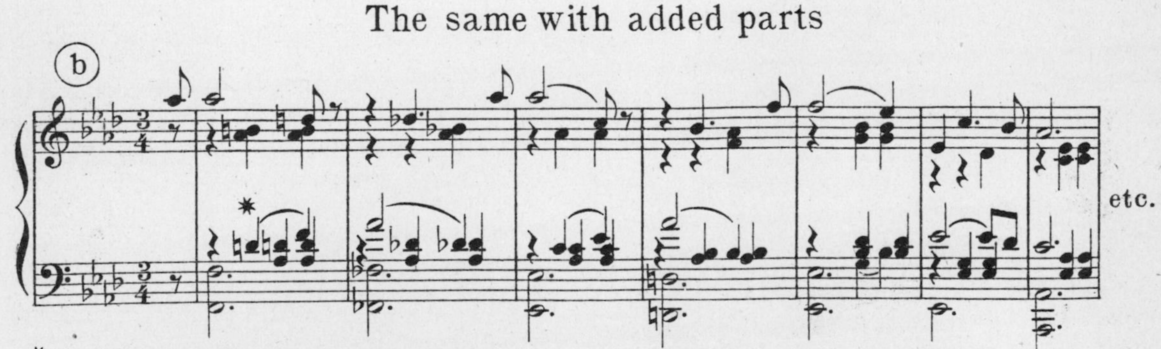

* Observe the melodic figure in slurred quarter and half notes.

In addition to the foregoing information and illustration, which deals with "filling in" or adding parts to piano solos selected for band arrangements, it may be well to mention that certain songs, waltzes, etc., require, for the clarinets and flutes, harmonic or melodic figuration arranged in the form of variations. Further, the euphonium, bassoon, and Alto and Bass clarinets, may sometimes be employed on the arpeggio style of accompaniment. In this connection a careful review of the closing chapters of "The Material Used in Musical Composition" by Goetschius, which deals with figuration and simple variation, is recommended.

EXERCISE VII

Select several piano solos, first, those that require added parts and thickening of the harmony, and arrange them for full band, following out the instruction given under Classification V; secondly, those that require a thinning out of the chords in close position that lie low on the band keyboard, and lastly, those that may be arranged for band without any changes in their construction. In this connection, a partial list of good compositions for arranging material is given:

A LIST OF PIANO SOLOS REQUIRING ADDED PARTS, Etc:

"Serenade Badine". . . . . .Gabriel-Marie.
"Gondolied". . . . . .Theo. Oesten.
"Serenade". . . . . .Pierne.
"Turkish March". . . . . .Mozart.
"Valse des Fleurs". . . . . .Ketterer.
"Valse Brillante". . . . . .Schulhoff.
"Kuhlau Sonatinas" for Piano (In two volumes)

A LIST OF PIANO SOLOS THAT REQUIRE THINNING OUT:

"Elsa's Wedding Procession". . . . .Wagner
(from "Lohengrin") Transcribed by Liszt.
"Colonial Song". . . . . .Grainger.
"Prelude in G Minor". . . . . . . .Rachmaninoff.

A LIST OF PIANO SOLOS THAT MAY BE ARRANGED FOR BAND WITHOUT ANY CHANGES IN THE CONSTRUCTION:

"Wedding March". . . . . .Mendelssohn.
"Prelude in C♯ Minor". . . . . . .Rachmaninoff.
"Morning" from "Peer Gynt Suite". .Grieg.
"Priest's March" (from Athalia) . . .Mendelssohn.

Four-hand arrangements for piano may be used to advantage in some instances.

APPENDIX TO PART II

(a) The Arrangement Of Light And Popular Music

The arrangement of light and popular music, such as military marches etc., require, generally, an application of the principles laid down under Classification V, page 58 (viz: arranging from Piano Music). In order to make creditable arrangements from musical compositions of this character, the student's ability to invent new and interesting parts; fill out the harmony etc., must be equal to that required for the arrangement of standard and classical works. However, music in popular style is scored more heavily and fuller thruout than is the case with more pretentious works. Therefore, the ingenuity of the arranger in the matter of variety and tonal shadings, is not called upon to any great extent.

In connection with the foregoing, the introduction and opening measures of a military march are here given for piano, followed by an arrangement for full Military Band.

It will be observed that an added part has been given to the Alto clarinet, Alto saxophone, 2nd and 3rd cornets and trombones in the 9th, 10th, 11th and 12th measures. In this particular illustration, the band parts have been scored a tone lower than the piano solo for the reason that the march, as a whole, is better adapted to the band in the chosen key. (The band arrangement of this march is published by Carl Fischer, Inc. N.Y.)

22998-73

"El Supremo" MARCH
65
Arranged for Full Military Band
W. C. WHITE
D♭ Piccolo
C Flutes
Oboes
E♭ Clarinet
Solo & 1st B♭ Clarinets 2nd & 3rd
Alto Clarinet
Bass Clarinet
Saxophones
Soprano
Alto
Tenor
Baritone
Bassoons
Solo & 1st B♭ Cornets 2nd & 3rd (or Trumpets)
E♭ Horns (Altos)
Baritones
1st & 2nd Trombones 3rd
Basses (Tubas)
Drums
Tympani
Bells
(Tacet)
22998-73

(b) Instrumentation And The Arrangement Of Instruments In The Score

While the instrumentation of Military Bands varies (especially in amateur organizations) to some extent, due to the fact that certain instruments are not always available, the instrumentations listed below, consisting of bands of 28, 36 and 48 men respectively, have been adopted by the U. S. Army and may be considered good models.

28 Men	36 Men	48 Men
1 Piccolo, D♭ } for 1 man.	1 Piccolo D♭ } for 1 man	1 Piccolo, D♭ } for 2 men
1 Flute, D♭	1 Flute, D♭	1 Flute, D♭
1 Flute, C	1 Flute, C	1 Flute, C
1 Clarinet, E♭	1 Oboe	2 Oboes
6 Clarinets, B♭	1 Bassoon	2 Bassoons
1 Saxophone, Tenor.	1 Clarinet, E♭	1 Clarinet, E♭
1 Saxophone, Alto.	7 Clarinets, B♭	10 Clarinets, B♭
1 Saxophone, Baritone.	1 Saxophone, Alto.	2 Clarinets, Alto.
4 Trumpets, B♭	1 Saxophone, Tenor.	2 Clarinets, Bass.
2 Cornets, B♭ (or flugelhorns)	1 Saxophone, Baritone.	1 Saxophone, Alto.
3 French horns.	4 Trumpets, B♭	1 Saxophone, Tenor.
1 Baritone or Euphonium.	1 Clarinet, Alto.	1 Saxophone, Baritone.
3 Trombones, B♭, slide.	1 Clarinet, Bass.	4 Trumpets
1 Bass, E♭	2 Cornets, B♭ (or flugelhorns)	2 Cornets, B♭ (or flugelhorns)
1 Bass, BB♭	4 French horns	4 French horns
1 Snare drum and Triangle.	1 Baritone, B♭	1 Baritone, B♭
1 Bass drum and Cymbals.	1 Euphonium	1 Euphonium
	3 Trombones, B♭, slide.	4 Trombones, B♭, slide.
	1 Bass, E♭	2 Basses, E♭
	2 Basses, BB♭	2 Basses, BB♭
	1 Snare drum and Triangle.	1 Sarrusophone, E♭
	1 Bass drum and Cymbals.	2 Snare drums
		1 Triangle
		1 Bass drum and Cymbals.

The arrangement of instruments in the score, as given below, has been universally recognized by composers and arrangers for Military Bands, viz:

Piccolo	Alto Saxophone	Baritones
Flutes	Tenor Saxophone	1st and 2nd Trombones
Oboes	Baritone Saxophone	3rd Trombone
E♭ Clarinet	Bassoons	Basses (Tubas)
B♭ Clarinets	B♭ Cornets and Trumpets	Drums
Alto Clarinet	Flugelhorns	Tympani
Bass Clarinet	1st and 2nd Horns (Altos)	Bells
Soprano Saxophone	3rd and 4th Horns (Altos)	

NOTE: Carl Fischer Inc. of New York deals in score paper with the instruments arranged according to the above model. The use of this paper is recommended to the Student.

(c) Tone Coloring

The term "tone coloring" implies a particular quality of tone obtainable from the military band by any special combination of instruments. While varieties of such coloring are used as a means of contrast, the two terms are not interchangeable. It is quite possible to get contrast without color and vice versa. For example, musical phrases or figures may have considerable contrast in the rhythmic structure, but, if they are written for either a clarinet choir or a brass combination the same "color" will obtain throughout. Again a most peculiar and beautiful coloring may be given to the band by employing a quartet of saxophones, or by the addition of alto and bass clarinet as well as certain double reed instruments, without producing any marked contrast.

There are no fixed rules for coloring, although a few general principles may be deduced from the practice of the best composers and illustrated by examples from their scores. The following excerpt from Auber's "Les Chaperons Blancs" shows that effective coloring may be obtained by employing the horns, bassoon, flugel horn and soprano saxophone on the sustained notes in the first nine measures of the extract. Also a certain brightness is acquired in the last four measures by doubling the first B♭ clarinet in the octave with a flute and E♭ clarinet.

22998 - 73

A brilliant color may be obtained by employing the more acute instruments (flute, B♭ clarinet, E♭ clarinet, etc.) in the high registers, taking care, of course, not to leave the inner harmonies too thinly scored. Brilliancy may be secured without employing the full band; as the following example from Meyerbeer's "Dinorah" (in short score) will show.

The notes given are at concert pitch, not as written for transposing instruments.

NOTE: By the addition of two small bells, sounding thrice lined f♯ much brightness is added to the passage. The doubling of the melody in the lower octave, first by the oboe and soprano saxophone and later by a flugelhorn, bridges over the wide gap between the flute, E♭ clarinet and solo B♭ clarinet, and other instruments carrying the harmony parts.

Somber color may be obtained by employing low reeds and other instruments in their middle or low registers and causing the high sounding instruments to be silenced. The Prelude to "Les Huguenots" by Meyerbeer, also Verdi's "Requiem," offer splendid examples of such scoring.

Other coloring depicting desolation, religious scenes, gaiety, horror, etc., may be secured by judicious employment of tympani, bells and other instruments of percussion. Many excellent examples of this kind may be found in the works of Mozart, Beethoven, Wagner, Verdi, Grainger, Rachmaninoff, and Franck.

(d) Contrasts

Many ways of obtaining contrasts are available in our present day, by reason of the variety of instruments now included in the instrumentation of military bands. The different groups (flute, single and double reed, brass and percussion) may be employed alternately, or the various members of one or more groups may be combined in many and varied forms. With clarinets alone, far more variety is possible than the student may imagine. Contrast, then, may be regarded as follows: (a) The contrasts of instruments employed simultaneously, and (b) the contrast of instruments employed in succession. The symphonies of Haydn offer many excellent examples of contrast and are recommended to the student for study. His "Military Symphony," published for military band by Carl Fischer Inc. New York, is well worth serious study and is by no means antiquated in so far as contrasts are concerned. The military band arrangement of Schubert's B minor Symphony (Unfinished) also contains several fine examples of contrast, especially in the first movement. Other good examples exist in the following works: Overture to "Merry Wives of Windsor" Nicolai, "Stabat Mater" Rossini, Overture to "Rosamunde" Schubert, etc.

An excellent example of a mixture of color and contrast from Auber's "Acteon" is given below. The sustained effect of the horns against the staccato of the other instruments is very noticeable, as is also the change of position in the last two chords; had they been the same as the first chord in the bar the last notes of the E♭ clarinet solo would not stand out so prominently. (The following extract is at concert pitch, not as written for transposing instruments).

"Acteon"

(e) The Combination Of The Concert Pipe Organ With The Military Band

While the Concert Pipe Organ is not a constituent of the orchestra, it has, since the days of Bach, been used in combination with Concert orchestras, large and small, especially in music of a sacred character or of pompous and dignified import.

The Military Band with its full complement of single and double reed, including besides the flute and piccolo, the E♭, B♭, Alto, Bass Clarinets, the Saxophone Choir and the Contra-Sarrusophone, is an excellent parallel to the concert pipe organ, and blends admirably with that instrument when used in combination with it. For the organ and orchestra we find many valuable works; such as the "Ode for St. Cecilia's Day" by Handel; the 4th. Mass of Haydn; the 14th. Mass of Mozart; Mendelssohn's 98th Psalm, etc., etc. No attempt however, has been made by arrangers or conductors to combine the organ with the military band, although it has been proved that such a combination is ideal and worthy of serious consideration.

A grand climax of band arrangements or passages requiring a broad and sustained effect furnishes excellent opportunity for the employment of the organ. Further, such works as Rheinberger's Organ Concerto Op. 137, with orchestra accompaniment, and Guilmant's 1st. Symphony for organ and orchestra may be transcribed for the military band and organ, and would be very effective. The modern military band deserved better recognition by musicians and composers than formerly obtained, and military band conductors should make every effort to have this recognition brought about, and thereby secure for bands their rightful place in the realm of music.

The closing measures of the Andante Maestoso from Liszt's Symphonic Poem "Les Preludes" for military band, also the Finale of Boito's "Mefistofele" offers excellent opportunity to employ the organ with the military band.

(f) Balance Of Tone As Applied To Military Band Arranging

In his early attempts the student arranger will experience quite some difficulty in securing a good balance of tone among the various band instruments, especially so in mixed combinations of reed and brass, for the reason that the variance in the quantity (as well as quality) of tone between the reed and brass instruments is great. For example, should a reed choir, with the addition of-- say a baritone and a horn--be allotted a certain passage in ensemble the brass instrument will be much more pronounced on the voice, or part, which it is to carry than it would be if played by a reed instrument.

Therefore, a knowledge of the tonal balance or degrees of power existing between all instruments, reed or brass, as well as the strong and weak registers of instruments, becomes a vital necessity.

This knowledge can best be gained by practical study of the instruments. However, if it be not possible to study each instrument individually, a treatise on band instrumentation should be sedulously studied. "The Wind Band and its Instruments", Clappé, "Modern Orchestration and Instrumentation," Kling, and "The Principles of Wind-Band Transcription," Clappé, are recommended to the Student for this purpose.*)

To illustrate this point, let the student begin with the Wood-Wind and Reed and carefully tabulate the *best* notes on each instrument, as well as the weak ones, and notes that are difficult to produce; for example: the registers of the B♭ clarinet and other instuments are illustrated in Part I of this work and show the various notes; weak, strong, difficult, etc.

After a sound knowledge of the compass and quality of tone of the different instruments has been acquired, the student should arrange the instruments for which he is scoring into choirs or family groups, viz:

Flute group.	Flutes and Piccolos
Clarinet Choir	E♭ Clarinet B♭ Clarinets Alto Clarinet Bass Clarinet
Double reed group	Oboes Bassoons
Saxophone quartet. . . .	Soprano Alto Tenor Baritone
Trumpet group.	Trumpets Trombones

*) The three works are published by Carl Fischer, Inc. New York.

Saxhorn and mixed group. . . .	Cornets Altos Baritones Basses Flugelhorn French Horn
Percussion group	Drums and traps Tympani Bells and Xylophone

If it is desired to score for quartet, the student must keep within the bounds of a quartet, not only as regards balance but register also.

A complete knowledge of the quality and strength of tone of individual instruments is the guide for a proper balance, and the entire compass of a group or family of instruments determines the extent of the register; for example: The Clarinet Choir has a compass of over four octaves and a fifth. (see Part I).

When scoring for a small mixed combination of reed and brass, the weaker, though more facile, reed instruments will require to be numerically greater than those of the brass, and so on.

In making full band arrangements the student should keep in mind the relative dynamic values of each choir or family of instruments and endeavor to score so that no part will be overbalanced.

The inability of young performers to read and play their parts properly often causes a grievous disturbance in the balance of tone. This, however, does not reflect discredit upon the arranger. His duty is to score carefully and intelligently for properly balanced organizations. The matter of a creditable performance is then left to the ability of the bandmaster and his band.

CONCLUSION

It is almost universally conceded that supplementary reading and study is necessary to gain a broad knowledge of any subject. With this in view, it is recommended that the student avail himself of the books referred to in the Introduction of this work, and any others that will tend to increase his knowledge of military band instruments and their use.

To be able to arrange for the military band, artistically, requires continuous practice, as has already been noted. This book is intended only for the novice and it is hoped that he may gain, from a proper application of the information herein contained, a solid foundation on which to build fine facility for excellent work upon the important subject of Military Band Arranging.